"This is a memoir of a tangled and difficult mother-daughter relationship that will compel you to read on. It is a mortal story of flawed people facing illness and life's end. There is nothing pietistic or saccharine here, but there are blessings as O'Donnell confronts these hard realities through creative sacramental practices and literary insight. This narrative of failure and forgiveness will provoke daughters of every stripe to reflect on their most primal relationship."

Dana Greene
Dean Emerita of Oxford College
Emory University

"Angela O'Donnell invites us to ponder the gratuity and importance of ordinary gestures amidst the silence and helplessness of accompanying loved ones through illness, intrusive memory, and death. Through her eyes we discover that the 'holy folly' we engage in at such times takes on a sacred poignancy that we already knew, but never imagined."

Rev. Mark Mossa, S.J.
Author of *Already There: Letting God Find You*

A SACRAMENTAL FAREWELL

❖

Mortal Blessings

ANGELA ALAIMO O'DONNELL

ave maria press AMP notre dame, indiana

Excerpts from *Meditations from a Movable Chair* by Andre Dubus, copyright 1998 by Andre Dubus, copyright 1999 by Vintage Books/Random House.

Chapter 7, "The Sacrament of Honor," is reprinted with permission in a modified version from "Good Grief" in the December 3, 2010, issue of *Commonweal*.

"A Blessing for My Mother," "Watching *Dirty Dancing* with My Mother," "Real Presence," and "Poem on Waking" are reprinted from *Waking My Mother*, copyright 2013 by Angela Alaimo O'Donnell, with permission from WordTech Communications.

© 2014 by Angela Alaimo O'Donnell

Founded in 1865, Ave Maria Press is a ministry of the United States Province of Holy Cross.

www.avemariapress.com

Paperback: ISBN-13 978-1-59471-408-5

E-book: ISBN-13 978-1-59471-409-2

Cover image © Thinkstock.com.

Cover and text design by Brian C. Conley.

Printed and bound in the United States of America.

Library of Congress Cataloging-in-Publication Data.
O'Donnell, Angela Alaimo.
Mortal blessings : a sacramental farewell / Angela Alaimo O'Donnell.
    pages cm
Includes bibliographical references.
ISBN 978-1-59471-408-5 (pbk.) -- ISBN 978-1-59471-409-2 (ebook)
1. Caregivers--Religious life. 2. Sacraments--Catholic Church. 3. Death--Religious aspects--Christianity. 4. Terminal care--Religious aspects--Catholic Church. 5. Care of the sick. 6. Caring--Religious aspects--Catholic Church. I. Title.
BV4910.9.O36 2014
259'.41--dc23
                                    2014012306

For Rose Ann and Charlene,
my sisters,
for Gregory and Louie,
my brothers,
and for
Marion Salvi Alaimo,
our mother.

Down, down, down into the darkness of the grave
Gently they go, the beautiful, the tender, the kind;
Quietly they go, the intelligent, the witty, the brave.
I know. But I do not approve. And I am not resigned.

—Edna St. Vincent Millay

Don't weep excessively for a deceased person.
There are three days for weeping,
Seven days for eulogizing,
Thirty days for mourning . . .
Beyond that God says,
"Don't be more merciful than I am."

—Rabbi Yehudah Hachasid

But we do not want you to be uninformed, brethren, about those who
are asleep, so that you will not grieve as do those who have no hope.

—St. Paul

CONTENTS

INTRODUCTION

In late December 2009 on a sunny Florida afternoon, my eighty-two-year-old mother stepped across my sister's kitchen, caught her foot on the hem of her pink bathrobe, and fell onto the ceramic tile floor. She landed with sufficient force to break her right hip instantly, the hip opposite the one she had broken ten years earlier and that had been successfully repaired.

This second break was much worse than the first. The intervening decade had weakened my mother's body and, truth be told, her mind. A lifelong habit of smoking had led to COPD (chronic obstructive pulmonary disease), and a similarly long habit of excessive drinking had rendered her major organs vulnerable. This accident, as well as the surgery that might have saved a healthier person, would prove catastrophic in her weakened condition. So began the steady, inexorable disintegration of my mother's living body, which would conclude with her death exactly forty-eight days later, on February 1, 2010.

In the course of those forty-eight days, my siblings and I were drawn repeatedly from the far-flung places we lived

(New York, Philadelphia, Colorado) to my mother's side like magnets to steel. Each time we landed and made our way to our mother's bedside, we found ourselves encountering a new stage in what we would eventually understand to be her dying. And each time we arrived, we were newly clueless as to how to deal with the latest round of medical complications as well as the increasingly volatile emotional firestorm in which we had been placed dead center.

As I look back on those days, I am struck by the many moment-by-moment decisions we were forced to consider. While I believe that many of the choices we made, words we said, and actions we took were preceded by a process of careful thought and reasoning, I am also aware of the fact that many of these decisions were made by heart rather than by mind. We were wandering through strange terrain, and while there were occasional signposts suggesting a direction we might take, there also seemed to be signposts pointing in precisely the opposite direction.

We knew we were not in control of the large-scale medical events that were befalling our mother, so perhaps it seems natural that we found ourselves trying to exercise control in smaller, though no less significant, procedures. As the doctors and nurses made their regular rounds, introducing new pieces of alarming information, we went about the business of caring for our mother—activities that ranged from simply sitting by her side to feeding her and amusing her, always trying to keep her mind off what lay beyond our understanding. Quite unconsciously, we devised rituals, methods of dealing with overwhelming difficulty, which were rooted in sacramental practices we had learned as children in a modestly observant Catholic family.

My Epiphany

In one of his essays, Catholic fiction writer Andre Dubus describes in loving detail the ordinary process of making sandwiches for his school-age daughters. At the time he wrote the essay, Dubus was wheelchair bound—the result of a roadside accident—and his limited range of motion required him to develop routine and sometimes elaborate methods for accomplishing simple tasks.

This element of difficulty that had been introduced into his daily life provided Dubus with a new vantage point from which to appreciate the effort that goes into ordinary actions. He sees them in terms of the practical ends they accomplish, but the extended duration and deliberateness of his method also allows him and his readers to see a greater meaning behind them. Thus, it strikes us as both wonderful and true when we arrive, along with Dubus, at the remarkable discovery that this daily task of feeding his children is a kind of sacrament: "A sacrament is an outward sign of God's love, they taught me when I was a boy, and in the Catholic Church there are seven. But, no, I say, for the Church is catholic, the world is catholic, and there are seven times seventy sacraments, to infinity."[1]

As a literature professor and longtime admirer of Dubus's writing, I had read, believed, and shared these words with my students for years. But during the forty-eight days in which I was engaged in the ordinary tasks of daily care for a dependent parent, I was able to *feel* the truth of what had been merely an intellectual understanding.

THE CATHOLIC IMAGINATION AND THE SACRAMENTS IN EVERYDAY LIFE

Most of us live our daily lives immersed in the ordinary world. Beset by many tasks and responsibilities, we work to accomplish what we can, and we often do this without a great deal of thought or deliberation. These daily habits enable us to function reasonably well, practically speaking, but they can also blind us to the extraordinary nature of our own lives.

In his wonderful book *The Catholic Imagination*, sociologist and Catholic priest Andrew Greeley reminds his readers that Catholic tradition offers human beings a more expansive vision of life:

> Catholics live in an enchanted world, a world of statues and holy water, stained glass and votive candles, saints and religious medals, rosary beads and holy pictures. But these Catholic paraphernalia are mere hints of a deeper and more pervasive religious sensibility which inclines Catholics to see the holy lurking in creation. As Catholics, we find our houses and our world haunted by a sense that the objects, events, and persons of daily life are revelations of grace.[2]

Greeley's observation enables us to see that the world in any given moment is, in and of itself, a sacrament—that is, a revelation of the presence of God. Holy objects or "sacramentals" hint at this presence of the divine in the ordinary, but an imaginative engagement of the world enlarges our ability to see that all objects are potentially holy—or "sacramentals"—as are all human activities and, most important, all human beings.

This book is an account of my family's gradual discovery of this sacramental vision as we cared for our ailing mother. My hope is that readers who find themselves in a situation similar to ours will discover the grace that can be, at times, difficult to find. In addition, the book is meant to suggest that this vision is available to us in any number of circumstances. We are all travelers, making our journey through the landscape of our lives. If we are attentive to the road we are walking, we become aware of that landscape as one that is full of signs and symbols, each of them pointing to a reality that lies beyond our limited vision.

Seen this way, every aspect of the stories of our lives becomes invested with meaning and importance—our childhood and upbringing, our parents and siblings, our education, our friends, our relationships to our spouses, our raising of our children, our life's work, our strengths and accomplishments, and our limitations and failures. What seems ordinary is not ordinary at all. Everything is, to use Greeley's term, "enchanted," charged with significance, and available to us as a manifestation of divine presence in our daily lives.

Perhaps I can illustrate some of the ways in which the seemingly simplest of actions can become charged with meaning when seen through the eyes of the sacramental imagination.

THE SACRAMENT OF PIE

The Latin word *sacramentum* is often translated as a "sign of the sacred." In the Catholic Church, sacraments are ceremonies that direct our attention toward the sacred by means of the mundane, toward the spiritual by means of the physical, toward the eternal by means of the transient. The priest uses bread and wine to signify (and, in Church teaching, through the mystery of transubstantiation, to *become*) the body and blood of Christ.

Similarly, in Baptism, the pouring of water over the infant's head signifies a ritual cleansing, bathing the child in the waters of life, and also the drowning of the old self and the emergence of the new—a process further signified by the new name the child receives. The words, the actions, and the material substances are all signs, aural and visible presences, of the invisible gift of grace. In addition, sacraments are communal in nature. They require participants and witnesses, effectively drawing us into communion with one another for the purpose of sanctification.

These elements of ritual, of material substances, and of communion were all present in the sacraments we shared with our mother. The rites we devised as we cared for her served a practical function—feeding her, keeping her spirits up, clothing and grooming her body—but they also served a transcendent one. They were, indeed, outward signs of invisible grace as well as mute testaments to the love we shared with one another—a human, familial love that is, ultimately, an expression of divine love. I was struck by this, even as we were performing these rituals in the ICU, in the hospital, in the nursing home and, finally, in her hospice room.

At the same time, I was struck by the humble and everyday nature of the materials we employed—not bread and wine, but pie and Ensure, and not chrism oil, but nail polish and scissors. Even so, the ordinariness of these substances seemed to underscore the deep significance of the actions we were engaged in.

A few weeks after her fall, my mother had rallied enough to undergo surgery and was moved to a nursing facility. This was a brief, hopeful period, a relief from the incessant worry. Each day and hour had its attendant rituals, but the one she enjoyed most was the evening visit. Nightfall occasioned the bringing of an offering (most often in the form of a store-bought Key lime pie). We would process into the room, announce the flavor of the pie, ceremoniously remove the clear plastic cover, cut a generous slice, place it on a plate, and feed it to my mother. She, in turn, would savor each bite, chewing the crust with some difficulty (since her dentures had been removed), uttering small, childish cries of delight, and then pronouncing how *"dee-LI-cious"* it was. She would wash it down with a sip from the pint-sized carton of Ensure, the fortified milk she was given to drink. We would repeat the feeding, receiving exactly the same response from her, and repeat the sip, until the first piece was consumed. And then we would cut another slice.

I was astonished, both then and now, by the force with which it hit me: this ritual was Eucharist by another name. Here I was, a child feeding my mother, our role reversal reminding me of the innumerable meals she had fed me in the course of my life, beginning with my life in utero and continuing into my adulthood. We had come full circle in the round of life we had led, and this ritual served to circumscribe the sacred, mysterious relationship between mother and child. It gestured toward our shared past even as it unfolded in the present moment. In addition, it pointed to the future as I realized that I, too, would be in her position one day, having my own children feed me.

It was all this and more. True, this action encompassed and indicated our common humanity (we all need to eat to live) and our common dependence upon one another, but it also gestured toward a greater, transcendent hunger that needs filling in the here and now. Our ordinary communion seemed a version of the divine Communion we celebrate at Mass, food for the body and the soul that originates in the infinite generosity of a God who came to live among us and who continually gives himself to us in order that we might have life.

There is something about the nearness of death that triggers such glimpses into the nature of life. Small actions that might be seen as burdensome, repetitive, and numbingly boring can suddenly become charged with mystery, freighted with history, and full of meaning we feel but find difficult to explain. Such epiphanies redeem the actions themselves but, more important, they serve to redeem the often fraught and fractured relationships between the people enacting these ordinary sacraments. Here, through the agency of pie, I was offering my mother everything I had unconsciously withheld from her for years: understanding, compassion, forgiveness and, yes, even love. In response to my offerings, her mantra of "delicious" served as her "Amen" and sounded to me like a series of acknowledgments: *I know*; *Thank you*; *I forgive you*; and, most moving of all, *I've always loved you*.

And so our ordinary Eucharist also served the purpose of another sacrament, an enacting of Confession, which was greeted with forgiveness and mutual absolution. My forgiveness of my mother (she had not been the best) entailed my forgiveness of myself for my own shortcomings as a daughter (I had not been the best). As for my mother, in her newfound simplicity of mind and heart, enjoying her pie received at the hands of her child, she had been miraculously relieved of any sense of guilt, resentment, or anger. In the face of extremity, all was forgiven.

These meals proved to be among her last, and so they proved to be mortal blessings: "mortal" in the sense that they do not—cannot—last, "blessings" in the sense that they impart benediction on both giver and receiver.

As Andre Dubus points out in "On Charon's Wharf," another of his essays, "we are all terminally ill."[3] All of us are engaged in the inevitable march toward our own mortality. But these sacramental moments enable us to pause in that march, to offer a gesture of love wherein we give ourselves away and thereby acquiesce to our common fragility and humanity. And this is, strangely, cause for both sadness and joy.

"Seven Times Seventy Sacraments, to Infinity"

In this book, I've set out to delineate the sacraments we take and the sacraments we make—placing the familiar ones we (as Catholics) receive in the course of our life in the Church beside the makeshift sacramental practices that we create in extreme circumstance. This sacramental attention and invention took a variety of forms in the course of the forty-eight days of my mother's illness; in the course of the funeral and burial ceremonies we planned and observed; and also in the days, weeks, and months of mourning that ensued.

This brief meditation on the "Sacrament of Pie" serves as an example of the many ways in which my family's attention to the illness, decline, death, and mourning of my mother took on the quality of sacrament. We perceived in these experiences signs of that enchanted world Fr. Greeley speaks of wherein every action takes on significance that is both local and transcendent. As the quotation from Dubus's essay suggests, there are many more of these sacraments, both small and large, than can be counted, so my goal is not so much to be exhaustive but, rather, to be suggestive of the possibilities. In addition, it is my hope that these specific moments in my family's lives, our makeshift sacramental practices, will enable the reader to see the many invitations to sacramental practice in his or her daily life, whether in moments of extremity or in moments of relative calm. Thus, the task of caring for an infant (one usually associated with joy) and that of caring for an aging parent (one usually associated with sorrow) might equally serve as occasions for meditation, a source of wisdom, and a goad to gratitude.

The book proceeds chronologically, cast as a series of linked narratives charting the course of my mother's final illness and the parallel course of my family's gathering of resources and strength in preparation for her passing. It chronicles her hospitalization, her time in the ICU, her surgery, her (brief) recovery in the nursing facility, and her last hours in hospice care. The final chapter of the book explores the sacramental elements (and lack thereof) of our attention to her cremation, her funeral, and her eventual interment.

Mortal Blessings is about the discovery and unfolding of these sacraments. Each chapter serves as an occasion for meditation on the details and significance of a specific practice and attempts to describe the ways in which each sacrament served and strengthened our family, with implications for all of our lives and situations. One of the discoveries we made during this experience is that engagement in the enchanted or sacramental world brings human beings closer together. Sacrament thrives in and creates community. Readers can likely attest to this discovery in their own lives as well: going through a trial by fire with another human being gives us someone to share the burden with and cements that relationship; we share an experience that is unique, intense, unrepeatable, and holy. This attests to one of many ways in which, paradoxically, suffering itself serves as a sacrament and a vehicle of grace.

Through these pages, the reader will encounter my family's story but also the words and thoughts of a range of voices on the subject of sacrament. Most of the voices are those of theologians, fiction writers, and poets—some are biblical voices as well. Their words provide precedents, articulations of fresh and sage ways to think about sacramentality—and give us permission to think creatively about it ourselves. The selection of writers is not reflective of a particular agenda; rather, it is a collection of writers who have influenced my own ever-growing understanding of the sacred.

A central challenge of writing this book has been to be as truthful as possible in recounting my family's particular experience of loss. Though we were all afflicted by immense sadness, we are, as a family, characteristically given to humor and irony. In part, this is because our family was stricken by a series of domestic disasters when we were children. Our father, who was chronically ill, died unexpectedly, widowing my young mother with five children; our eldest brother suffered a brain tumor and nearly died six months later; and a close family friend, a man my mother loved very much, died in a terrible car accident a few years afterward. Scarred as we were by these events, humor helped us to cope then, and it continues to help us cope now. I mention this by way of differentiating between humor that is irreverent and humor that is human and enables us to endure.

At times, the circumstances require me to reveal personal details of our family life (my mother's alcoholism, for example). I do this when necessary and only when it serves the purpose of elucidating the range of possibility for "seven times seventy" sacramental practices. I also include these details as a way of acknowledging that no family is perfect—neither the writer's nor the reader's—and that it is our uniquely human condition to live in a state of imperfection. In fact, amending those imperfections is one of the functions of sacrament.

These rituals of love are a gift, and the practice of them gives us the opportunity to become better people.

Though the actors in this story and the particular details involved are specific to my family, scenarios such as those I recount are unfolding in hospitals, homes, and nursing facilities across the world at this very moment. Ours was—and is—an experience both local and universal and as such, it is meant to be easily recognizable to anyone who has cared for a sick or dying parent.

My hope is that readers who share the difficult and painful experiences associated with the loss of a loved one might find in them the ritual patterns and redemptive qualities of sacrament, that they might derive some solace from the fact that they are not alone, and that they might arrive at a fuller understanding of the powerful and pervasive role ritual and sacramental practice play at key moments in our lives, even (and, perhaps, especially) when we are least aware of it.

Chapter 1

THE SACRAMENT OF SPEECH

In the beginning was the Word . . .
And the Word was made flesh, and dwelt among us.
—John 1:1, 14

"In the beginning was the Word." This is the celebrated opening line of the Gospel of John. The Word here—or *logos* in
Greek—refers to Christ and describes the Son of God as a
being who has always coexisted with God, who has no beginning and no end, and who lives beyond and outside of time.
Later the gospel tells us that "the Word was made flesh, and
dwelt among us." The Word did not remain a disembodied
power or energy source. (And, if we think about it, this is
what ordinary words are.) Instead, the Word became an in-
carnate being in the world, one who could share in human
existence and know birth and death, our sufferings and our
joys, our weaknesses and our strengths, firsthand. Thus, the
Word reveals and embodies God's presence in the world.

This scripture passage describes the miracle of the Incarnation, and it also reminds us of the primacy of the word or of language. The Bible begins with the story of creation. God proclaimed a set of words, "Let there be light," and there was light. Thus, the world is literally spoken into being. Words are accorded enormous power throughout the Bible. The prophets and patriarchs are given words for God's people to live by, and Jesus frequently quotes these words to his followers, reminding them of the importance of Holy Writ: "'Man shall not live on bread alone, but on every word that comes from the mouth of God" (Mt 4:4).

Words, then, are a source of creative energy, of revelation and, at times, of destructive power. In addition to being tools that we need in order to think and speak and accomplish ordinary tasks, words constitute a sign for us to read, to pay attention to, and to use with discretion and wisdom in terms of the sacramental vision. Saints know this, as well as sinners. It is no accident that the first directive of the *Rule* of St. Benedict, the handbook Benedict designed for his monks, derived from the book of Proverbs, is to "listen with the ear of your heart."

Words also have a primacy in our own lives as well as in Judeo-Christian religious tradition. For most of us, the first words we hear—whether in utero or after we are born—are spoken to us by our mothers. We learn language from them (hence the term "mother tongue"), we practice speech within the community of our families, and then we go out into the world equipped with a grammar and vocabulary, speech rhythms and intonations, and (if we're fortunate) a sense of language as a powerful instrument necessary for us to live a rich and satisfying life. Our way of speaking identifies us with the clan we come from, with a region, with an ethnic group, and with a social class. Yet our way of speaking is also highly individualized. No two siblings speak in exactly the same way. Thus, language serves as an oral and aural version of our fingerprint. We all use language in unique and interesting ways, yet we use it, mostly, for the same purpose: to communicate—and thereby to create community—with others. So it makes sense to begin an inquiry into the sacraments we make with the Sacrament of Speech.

THE POWER OF WORDS

I grew up in a family in which words mattered, and we five children took a particular delight in language as an instrument of power (this is how one gained the upper hand in an argument); a means of getting attention (our household was noisy and frenetic); and a source of delight (we loved jokes, wordplay, prevarication, and myth-making of all kinds).

This facility with words set us apart, in fact, from our more practical parents. The children of Italian immigrants, neither my father nor my mother had more than a high school education, and neither was especially interested in academic pursuits. My father was a factory worker. My mother was a housewife and busy mother, and she also worked evenings and weekends as a waitress. Words aided them in accomplishing the practical tasks associated with their labors and provided them with a means for simple conversation, mostly with and among people they knew well. For them, language was almost entirely an oral and aural experience. By this, I mean that they were not readers; they did not engage the silent, written word very often and therefore didn't share in the experience of inhabiting the multiple worlds of words that reading provides.

In addition, both of my parents were raised in bilingual households. This meant that English was reserved for purely practical expression. Anything of deeper significance would be conveyed in Italian or in the Sicilian dialect.

My siblings and I were shaped by American culture in a variety of ways. We enjoyed better schooling than my parents had access to and therefore learned to read and write English with greater skill and efficiency. We were exposed to different kinds and modes of speech through the growing presence of television, radio, popular music, and daily communication with people outside of the small circle of immediate family. Our collective world was bigger than that of our parents, in every sense of that word. As a result, we learned early on that speech and language served multiple purposes in multiple settings and circumstances, and we enjoyed adapting our speech to those situations and using words in inventive ways, naturally and unselfconsciously.

Another enormous influence on our sense of language was the experience of growing up Catholic. As a child, I found it interesting that my mother regularly had difficulty spelling and pronouncing everyday words correctly, yet when we went to Mass she could recite the elevated and archaic language of the Creed and the noble poetry of the Our Father without a single glitch. I used to wonder how the woman who would consistently misspell "lettuce" (as "lettis") on a store list could sing the words—and the notes—of "Holy God, We Praise Thy Name" with perfection: "Infinite thy vast domain, / Everlasting is thy reign." I had no idea what those words meant—and I was pretty sure my mother didn't know either—but they succeeded in lifting our minds out of the ordinary and the superficial toward the unseen, transcendent world that lay beyond us.

In such moments, we learned and practiced speech as sacrament. Praying these words and rhythms in unison unleashed, somehow, a mysterious power. Through the familiar cadences and constructions of words we heard at Baptisms, weddings, funerals and, on a more frequent basis, at the consecration of the Eucharist, we quietly absorbed the Catholic fact that words are efficacious. They enabled us to accomplish serious, consequential things. Words enabled us to confess our iniquity, and they also absolved us from our sins. They turned ordinary bread and wine into the body and blood of Christ and enabled us to partake of divinity. They snatched souls from limbo and set them on a course toward heaven. They invited the Holy Spirit to inhabit our bodies and our souls. They turned ordinary men into priests and ordinary women into nuns. Through their strange magic, they enabled two people to become one, so thoroughly united that the two could not be put asunder.

If words had so much power in church, our post–Vatican II minds reasoned, they must retain some of that power beyond the church walls. Just as God is everywhere (as we learned in after-school catechism class), so is the Word.

This Catholic attitude toward language enabled us, even as children, to see words as potentially powerful and efficacious in everyday life. Not that we were always conscious and respectful of that power—we abused words along with everyone else, often outrageously so. (Name-calling was a favorite sport, infinitely preferable to physical fighting. A well-chosen name could strike home as a mere fist to the face could not.) But we were also sensitive to sound and took special note of the way people spoke, noticing their accents and tonalities and their odd expressions. Somehow we knew that the way a person spoke was deeply revelatory of who he or she was. You could "read" a person's heart by listening. Perhaps this is why we five children paid such close attention to our mother's speech.

OUR MOTHER'S TONGUE

Marion Salvi Alaimo was petite, attractive, and possessed a lively spirit—a *bon vivant* who loved nothing so much as a party. This quick sketch describes my mother as she was at twenty-one, when she made a hasty and wise marriage to Charles Alaimo, the man who would become our father (she was already expecting my eldest brother), and as she was at eighty-one, the age she reached before she died. Her long years of smoking and excessive drinking, along with the inevitable effects of aging, had surely dampened her youthful energy and compromised her beauty, but these qualities were so foundational to her personality that, for us, she never really lost them. The old, young Marion was always there, just beneath the surface, and would flare up in unpredictable, brief bursts of flame. These glimmers of her former self would arrive almost invariably in the form of her speech. Such moments, especially those that took place in the sick room during her final forty-eight days, brought us joy, for we recognized in them a kind of grace. Illness and mortality rob us of many things, but the core sense of who we are still persists if we attend closely enough to read the signs.

Conversation with my mother was often hilarious, and accidentally so. She would attempt to use common expressions and manage, somehow, to get them wrong in a multitude of ways. She would call everyday objects by the wrong name (peppers were "mangoes") and misread the labels on household products (Herbal Essence shampoo was "Herbal Adolescence"—with the initial "h" pronounced loudly). I remember an instance wherein our family was involved in a fender bender in center-city Philadelphia. When the police officers arrived on the scene, my frantic mother insisted that they call "AA" right away. She meant, of course, AAA, the roadside-assistance agency—not Alcoholics Anonymous—but the police didn't know that. I leapt into the conversation repeatedly, trying to clarify her request for them. (Happily, alcohol was not involved in the accident—this was before her real struggle with drinking had begun. Now, as I think back on it, her error seems strangely prophetic.)

Our mother was also very direct and colorful in her speech. She did not mince words. If she thought one of us was overweight—and as children of an Italian-American family in which food was inextricably bound up with love, we often were—she would tell us so. I recall sitting at the dinner table partaking of the plentiful meal she had set before us when I felt her eye fixed on me. When I looked up, she nodded knowingly and said just six words in the voice she reserved for the most wounding sarcasm: "Keep eating, Angela. Just keep eating." (Forty years later, I hear those words as I sit down to a meal. Though they pained me as a child, they have become a reliable internal warning system to help me keep my appetite and my weight in check. They work as no gentle euphemism or esteem-building assurance would have.)

But as surely as our mother could be judgmental and even—at times—cruel in her speech, she was our fiercest advocate. Whenever she learned that a teacher or employer had treated any of us unjustly, her favorite threat was the promise to "march into his office and wipe the floor up with him." We trembled at these words, hoping she would attempt no such thing and thereby add to our injury the humiliation of embarrassment. (Our five-foot-two mother could not wipe the floor up with anybody.) At times, she would actually call the offender, taking our side and thereby letting us know she was there for us, but most of the time the bluster was enough. Merely announcing the threat supplied us all with the mental picture of our petite mother as champion. This was immensely satisfying in its way. Once again, words were efficacious and justice—of a kind—was accomplished.

OUR FAMILY FALL

When my mother fell in December 2009, with her individual fall came our collective "Fall." My siblings and I fell from a state of midlife innocence into the experience of the reality of our seemingly unsinkable mother's mortality. The unspoken, irrational, childlike conviction that our resilient mother, who had recovered from every tragic loss and every illness that life had thrown at her, was somehow immune to death would come to an abrupt end within the next two months. She had made it through her own illnesses as well as multiple tragedies: my father's premature death at age forty-three, which had forced us all to become collectively self-sustaining; the following year, a brain tumor nearly killed my eldest brother and left him disabled; and some years later, a tragic car accident killed the man she had hoped might become her second husband. Given the trials she had weathered, it is little wonder we thought her indestructible. In a matter of months, we fell from the familiar state of being adult children of a difficult, headstrong mother (the words *spitfire* and *pistol* come to mind) into the unfamiliar state of being adults in charge of a weak and stricken woman who had been rendered a child again.

The story of the original Fall of Adam and Eve recounted in Genesis tells of a terrible new dispensation wherein human life in an eternal paradise comes to an end and a much-diminished life begins—one that holds no guarantee other than the inevitability of death. It was on such a threshold that we found ourselves. And like Adam and Eve, our first parents, we had no choice but to walk the journey that lay ahead. As John Milton writes at the end of his brilliant account of the Fall in *Paradise Lost*, "The World was all before them."[1] And so it was for us—and still is.

My mother's fall was precipitated by alcohol. (Indeed, she had been falling down and out of life on account of alcohol for decades.) It is often said that one dies as one lives—and this sober observation has the sad ring of truth to it. She had just come out of alcohol rehabilitation and was beginning to feel well again. Truth be told, Mom had been in and out of rehab for years, and each time she emerged, the same pattern would repeat itself: a few weeks of aversion to alcohol, followed by a few weeks of relative wellness and peace of mind, followed by the gradual return of her old anxieties and sorrows, followed by a momentary slip—the quick drink to remedy her sadness—followed by the inevitable descent into an ancient, ingrained habit.

Each time she would emerge from the program, she—and we—would be newly hopeful that this time the old pattern would not hold. In December 2009, she was at the tipping point yet again. She took that first drink, as she had so many times before—only this time, the drink proved immediately disastrous.

Why our mother fell, after just one drink, we do not know. Perhaps her body, compromised after years of heavy alcohol consumption, could not properly process it now. Perhaps it interacted with one of the many medications she was taking.

Or perhaps her long pink robe simply got in her way as she took that fatal step across my sister's kitchen.

It is a common piece of wisdom that of the interrogatives *who? what? when? where? why?*, the last one poses the most perplexing question. Not only is it the most difficult to answer, but it also opens the door to its follow-up question—one that often brings pain in the aftermath of disaster—*what if?* To question why seems to give us permission to judge, to look back with twenty-twenty hindsight, to accuse and to lay blame on others and on ourselves. The fact is my mother fell, and her fall was the result of many possible causes, some of which were potentially preventable but most of which were not. One thing we can be certain of is that her fall partook, in some way, of that original Fall. The fault or tragic flaw lies, paradoxically, both within and beyond all of us, from Adam and Eve on down.

REDEMPTION AND THE WORD

In Judeo-Christian tradition, there is no cure for the Fall. It cannot be undone or erased. There is no second chance for Adam and Eve, no retake in which they get it right. The Fall was precipitous, tragic, and enormously consequential, doomed to be repeated by the human beings who would come after, over and over and over again. That fateful action taken by the original human beings in the story—the choice of sin over love—called for a reversal of that action to be taken by future human beings—the choice of love over sin. According to Christian belief, the Incarnation serves as God's response to Adam and Eve; the birth, ministry, and sacrificial death of Christ reverse the effects of the first human sin, redeeming us all from death and promising life. If the Fall can be seen as humankind's tragedy, the redemption is the central act in the play of cosmic history, changing the conclusion of the drama, bringing life out of death, and rendering the play a comedy at last—not comedy in the sense of being humorous, but comedy in the classic sense of repairing damaged relationships, creating harmony out of disharmony, and bringing out of dire events a happy, joyful conclusion.

This redemption is a single event in time, but—like the original Fall—it is also ongoing. We are constantly falling (and failing) in a myriad of ways, and we are constantly being redeemed (and forgiven) in a myriad of others. One of the primary means of—as well as a sign of—our redemption is the use of resources available to us to commit acts of love. Included among these acts are the corporal works of mercy, and prominent among these is visiting the sick and, by implication, caring for them.

Care of the sick takes many forms, ranging from the dispensing of life-sustaining food, water, and medication to simply spending time in the presence of the suffering person. Among those listed, perhaps the latter duty is the most challenging. While it may not be difficult knowing what to feed a sick person (he or she is often on a carefully specified diet) or what medications to give (these are prescribed), knowing how to simply *be* in the presence of someone sick or struggling is something all of us must figure out on our own. When we were caring for our mother in the hospital and in the nursing home, it wasn't always clear how we ought to conduct ourselves and, most important, how we ought to *talk* to her. How we speak *to* and *for* and *about* the sick person has enormous significance, both for the body and for the spirit. Navigating this question—on a day-to-day, hour-to-hour, and minute-by-minute basis—over the course of forty-eight days provided insight for us into the Sacrament of Speech. We were able to discover the ways in which speech could be powerfully efficacious, not only in terms of accomplishing necessary practical communication but also in promoting comfort, peace, and healing in our mother and in ourselves. We also discovered the ways in which speech served the sacramental purpose of helping us to create community among ourselves, as my mother's children, giving us a common sense of purpose—and with the health-care professionals who were caring for her as well.

Speaking for Our Mother

When my sister Charlene called to tell me the terrible news—that Mom had fallen, had fractured her hip, and was unconscious in the ICU at Indian River Hospital—I was in my office in the Bronx at Fordham University preparing to give a final exam to my students. Fortunately, I was able to extricate myself from end-of-semester duties within thirty-six hours and catch a flight out of New York. My first thought when I walked into the ICU and saw my mother lying on her hospital bed was, "How tiny she is!" From a distance, with the ventilator mask covering much of her face and her head turned toward the far wall, one could have mistaken her for a child. In addition to being diminished in size by this trauma, she was also rendered speechless. Even on those occasions when her struggle for each breath was less intense and they could momentarily remove the oxygen mask, she would try to speak but could do so only incoherently. Robbed of air, of the ability to communicate, and of the drug that her body depended on (the ICU staff quickly figured out that Mom was in alcohol withdrawal, her weeks in rehab notwithstanding), we became the means of translating and communicating her needs. During the hours we spent with her, we became keenly aware of the modes of speech we were engaging in with her, with one another, and with the members of the hospital staff. Language became a lifeline for all of us as we struggled to understand her medical predicament and exercise some measure of control over it.

This desire for control is universal—all people who have dealt with a sick child or parent have clamored to get the upper hand of an illness or disease—and control is also an illusion. One of the lessons we quickly learned was that each new doctor and new technician told a different story, offered a different version of what was happening to my mother. They all agreed on a few basic facts: that her hip had been badly broken, that her organs were failing, and that she was not strong enough to survive the surgery necessary to keep her alive. Some of them believed that all of this added up to one thing: she was dying. Because of this, surgery was not only contraindicated (a fancy hospital term for a bad idea), but it would be a futile attempt to save a patient who was not savable (that "patient," another hospital term, would be our mother).

As my sisters and I sat with her, pondering this impossibility for the next several hours, another doctor crossed the threshold of her room, greeted us hastily, and took down her chart from the foot of the bed. His version of her situation was very different: not only was she not dying, she was eminently savable. In fact, allowing her to lie here in pain like this (despite heavy doses of powerful pain medications) without repairing the hip was shockingly cruel. As soon as her vital signs stabilized (more hospital terms), he was going to reserve a spot in the operating room for her. He then breezed out. (For the record, we never did see him again.)

And so began this waiting game, this surreal version of *Let's Make a Deal* wherein we were trying to decide whether Door 1 or Door 2 would yield the coveted prize: my mother's life. With each new doctor on duty came another (quick) prognosis, and each new technician and ER nurse would wager on which of the doctors was right, sometimes contributing her own theory based on years of observing this very scenario played out over and over again.

Where is the Sacrament of Speech in all of this, one might ask? Surely not in the "hospital speak." One of the observations my sisters and I could not help but make is that some of the staff spoke about my mother in human terms, while others spoke about her only in hospital terms, with a kind of cold, clinical detachment. Because of this, we were especially grateful to those nurse technicians, in particular, who would engage in genuine conversation with us and even with our barely conscious mother as they took care of her.

One woman I remember vividly was a night nurse. She was unusually sensitive to the agonies of our mother's alcohol withdrawal. Evidently, her own parents suffered from alcoholism, which made her sympathetic toward our mother's suffering. At one point, after the withdrawal was quite far along and my mother seemed to be experiencing *delirium tremens*, she confided in us that she kept a bottle of gin on the premises so that when alcoholic patients were brought into the ER, she might ease their withdrawal with a minute amount. "They are dealing with enough trauma," I recall her saying. "My job is to ease people's pain, not to help them get sober." (My sisters and I were shocked by this confession at first, but she assured us that she did this only after securing the permission of the physician treating the patient.) After this, I could not help but think of her as a rare kind of hospital angel, ministering to the deepest needs of her charges without prejudice and with a kind of practical love.

This nurse technician also practiced sacramental speech in asking us questions about our mother and listening to the answers. She showed genuine interest in our family dynamics, in the story of Mom's life, and in the circumstances of her fall. She comforted our fears and concerns, assuring us that she had seen many people in Mom's condition who had recovered. Her concern for Mom's well-being also showed itself in the way she interacted with my mother. Rather than treating our mother as an inanimate object when she bathed her, administered her medication, and took her pulse or temperature, this nurse looked at her, handled her gently, and spoke to her, remarking on the fine color of her hair (which retained its natural black until her death) and the smoothness of her skin. With such speech, motivated purely by kindness, she did more than simply communicate practical information to my mother—she acknowledged my mother's humanity; the common condition shared by women (the universal desire to look one's best, even in a hospital bed); and the dignity we all possess as human beings, whether in a weakened condition or a strong one.

SPEAKING TO OUR MOTHER

Our own attempts at conversation with our mother were motivated by similar desires. In addition, we wanted to encourage her, to give her information about her condition that might benefit her and, most of all, to distract her from her pain and her terror. Given this, much of our speech consisted of the details of ordinary life: what we had eaten for lunch or for dinner, what her grandchildren were doing this evening, and what the weather outside was like. We had no idea how much of this small talk our barely conscious mother could understand. We were also aware that our famously impatient mother was as likely to be irritated with our chatter as she was likely to be amused or interested. Yet we kept on talking.

It strikes me, as I place myself back in that room and listen to the three of us banter, that it was a kind of elaborate play, a show of bravado in the face of the unknown, staged entirely for my mother's benefit. It was a kind of ritual practice—as is all conversation, to some degree—meant to convey information, yes, but also designed to enact the unique relationships we shared. Beneath our surface banter, these were the deep messages we sent: *No matter what is happening to you and to us, we are still your daughters and you are still our mother. In the face of enormous change, these constants are not and cannot be altered.* Though we did not speak it as directly as she, our presence was a promise and a threat: that we would "wipe the floor up" with sickness and death—that there is no way either would win. *Just look how normally we're going about our lives, as if nothing is the matter,* our presence said. In the words of the old American spiritual, we might as well have chanted, "We shall not be moved."

One more element of the sacramental that characterized our speech to our mother throughout the course of her illness was the constant presence of humor. It may seem strange, in the face of suffering and amid the threat of death, to make jokes and to laugh. (In fact, the Sacrament of Humor is so strange and complex that it needs a chapter unto itself, so I'll speak only briefly about it here.) Because our relationship with our mother had always been marked by humor, by gentle teasing, and by exchange of insults (most of them gentle, some of them not), our conversation with her in the ICU was marked by these as well.

One particular—and potentially shocking—instance comes to mind. When our mom was going through alcohol withdrawal, on those occasions when we would remove her mask, she would ask quite insistently for a drink. At first, we assumed she meant water, but when we wetted her lips with the sponge given to us for that purpose, she spat it out. The first time this happened, we asked her what she wanted to drink, and the woman whose speech had previously been incomprehensible responded quite loudly and clearly, "I want some bourbon!" My sister, who knew my mother's habits and predilections, responded instantly: "But Mom, you don't like bourbon." Without missing a beat, our mother, high-handed and haughty as ever, set her straight, "Well, I like it now!"

We all laughed. Here was our mother, barely able to breathe, asking for a drink of the stuff that had nearly killed her (both slowly and quickly)—a scene that might be regarded as pathetically sad by many people, "a sign of the degrading effects of alcohol," etc., etc., etc. But we were so grateful for that spark of wit, that little flame of humor coming from this terribly sick woman, a sign that the headstrong old Marion (yes—*spitfire, pistol*) was still in there, well enough to yell at her daughters for not giving her what she wanted. And so this little exchange became a ritual. Whenever we would remove the mask, and whenever she would reject the water and ask for a drink, we would repeat the same dialogue, each of us playing our part. I cannot explain how unreasonably joyful that made us—and how unreasonably joyful it makes me even now as I remember it.

SPEAKING *ABOUT* OUR MOTHER

The final form of sacramental speech is the one that is most lasting, the one that is, in fact, still ongoing, even as I write these words. When my mother lost the ability to speak for herself, I soon realized that the responsibility of telling her story—both in the immediate present and for the future—had suddenly fallen to us. We were the witnesses to her suffering, we were the conveyers of her needs to the hospital staff and of her pain to our family, and we were the makers of the *mythos* by which her life (from start to end) would be passed on and understood.

It has been said of works of literature that the ending of a narrative confers meaning on the whole.[2] One cannot hope to understand the significance of a story or a novel, a play or a movie, or a poem or a song until one arrives at the end. The meaning of all that comes before is shaped by the conclusion. The ending provides context, connection, and closure. Loose ends are tied up, events foreshadowed actually occur (or not), and one has a sense of the role each action of the past plays in the person's future. The same might be said of a life. Even though we hoped—and expected—that our mother would survive her ordeal, we recognized this as a genuine moment of truth in her life, one that would have consequences, one that was packed with potential significance, and one that might very well constitute the beginning of the end; and it was our role (and privilege) to bear witness to that moment and all that it might mean.

Because of this realization, our conversations about our mother became weighted with unprecedented importance. We stored up and treasured moments of insight and eagerly shared them with one another, knowing but not speaking the truth we knew: that these might be among our last shared experiences with her. I wrote many of these moments down (writing being another form of speech), both in my journal and in poems that I began to compose about my mother. Even these words in this account participate in this Sacrament of Speech—the myth-making by which readers who never knew my mother are reading her story, coming into contact with her through the miracle of the word, even now. This is efficacious language, striving to put those of us living in (seemingly) ordinary time on the (seemingly) ordinary earth in touch with the eternal truth about ourselves as human beings, making us aware of our communion and of the divine heritage and destiny we share. This is the Sacrament of Speech, redeeming us all, moment by moment, word by Word, from the fall and from the Fall.

FELIX CULPA ("FORTUNATE FALL")

The Latin term *felix culpa* (translated as "fortunate fall") expresses the theological concept that the world is so pervaded by grace that this grace makes itself manifest even in the midst of disaster. Adam and Eve's Fall was a catastrophic event in salvation history, but their actions created the necessity of the Incarnation, the incursion of God into the world of human beings. The coming of the Son of Man (who was also the Son of God) redeemed their sin and our collective sorrow, restoring hope to humankind. There is deep beauty and wisdom in this formulation, since it offers testimony to the belief that evil cannot defeat goodness and death cannot overcome life, no matter what.

Though it is difficult to find grace in the suffering of those whom we love—especially when it is taking place before our eyes—sacramental practice makes the brief flashes of this pervasive grace evident. Sacrament is enacted ritual wherein the unseen is made visible, the unsayable is spoken, and the eternal is made manifest in the transitory world. All three of these conditions would be fulfilled, at various times, during Mom's forty-eight days in the ICU, nursing home, and hospice care. This sacramental practice, the attempt to heal disaster through redemptive acts of love, was set in motion by the split-second event of my mother's fall on December 16 at 5:00 p.m. in my sister's kitchen. It has yet to stop.

Chapter 2

THE SACRAMENT OF DISTANCE

It avails not, neither time or place—
distance avails not; I am with you.
—**Walt Whitman, "Crossing Brooklyn Ferry"**

Distance is defined as the physical space that separates two objects or persons, usually expressed numerically and in units of measurement. It is also a powerful metaphor for the emotional, intellectual, and spiritual space that intervenes between people. We often use the expression "I was miles away" to indicate our lack of attention to the present moment. Interestingly, we typically invoke the idea of distance as a negative—as if physical separation implies emotional separation and detachment. A person who is unfriendly or off-putting might be described as "distant," and we tend not to feel affection for distant people. In some sense, they are absent from us.

Yet distance can also provide us with perspective. We might consider the art of photography. When we are too close to the subject we are trying to photograph, we lose the background, the surrounding context that helps us locate it in space and time. If we back up and widen our focus, then we can see where the object is situated and appreciate it more fully in its proper setting. We might also be able to discern the time of day or the season of the year and to appreciate it in the context of time. A distant prospect also enables us to envision the object as a whole, rather than seeing merely its parts. This is particularly true if one is trying to photograph a large and imposing object. To get the whole of Mt. Etna in one's viewfinder, one has to stand at a great distance indeed.

This duality of the concept of distance became very important to me during my mother's final illness. For much of my life, I lived more than a thousand miles away from her. I would like to say this was mere happenstance—the result of the jobs my husband and I had landed—an accident of geography. But, if I were to be honest with myself, I would have to admit that I was grateful for the physical separation. For many years, it enabled me to remain detached from my mother's problems, while my sisters, in particular, had to witness them—and try to do something about them—every day. Distance afforded me the luxury of living my own life. I have met many other people in exactly my situation over the years, some of whom have become my dear friends. Most of us have made our choices deliberately—and most of us feel some measure of guilt.

For a long time, distance had been a gift that gave me freedom, but during my mother's illness it became an obstacle, a difficulty that had to be acknowledged and overcome, as well as a source of sorrow. Yet in the midst of this wrestling with distance, I found some measure of consolation in it, a perspective I would not otherwise have had, and so it served as a sacrament for me. As St. Ignatius teaches us, God is in all things. Distance gave me a means of seeing the many forms love and presence might take in the world.

PRACTICING DISTANCE

That my mother endured for forty-eight days after her fall, despite the condition of her body, is a testament to her strength and persistence. When I boarded that first flight to Florida after my sister's call, I believed it highly probable that she would not survive. These are the words I wrote in my journal just after the plane took off at 1:30 p.m. on December 18:

> My mother prepares for her journey. Lying on a bed of pain, breathing only with the help of machines—two knees hobbled, a broken hip, her lungs unable to swell and empty on their own—she is a husk. The life—her life—has begun to drain from her.
>
> I am on my way to be with her during these last hours. My sisters are at her side, faithful, faithful. She has been a difficult burden for so long. Who knows if we'll know how to walk upright after so many years? Perhaps we'll find she was not so heavy after all.
>
> Beneath me is a sea of clouds. It seems substantial, but I know it is only air, water—two of the four elements—and neither of them firm enough to put your foot upon.
>
> I watch the planes prepare to depart on the runway. Each glides, shining in the sun, and makes the last turn before the final takeoff. Then the engine

guns; she lifts and goes off. One after another. Like us.

Rereading these words, I am struck by how accurately I imagined my mother's predicament, even before I arrived to see her, how quickly I had begun to accept the possibility of her death, and how I had already started to imagine what life would be like without her. I am also struck by the lack of panic, the relative calm of these observations, and my acceptance of the inevitable as, well, inevitable.

This strange detachment has some connection, I'm sure, to the fresh point of view one acquires traveling thirty thousand feet above earth, freed (if only temporarily) from the limited range of vision one has at ground level. Such distance allows us perspective to see ourselves and those around us as part of a grand scheme—one that lies beyond our capacity to comprehend. This scheme is a kind of metaphor for the invisible, transcendent world we are unknowing participants in. At a distance, one can be thoughtful, theological, and faithful.

I would board a total of six flights between Florida and New York during the weeks of my mother's illness. Spending so many hours in the air, suspended between heaven and earth, loosed me from the gravitational pull of daily life, giving me the freedom and mental space in which to think, to write, and to pray.

In addition to this suspension in space, I was also suspended in time. Fall semester had ended and spring semester had not yet begun, meaning that my attention to my mother's situation was focused and nearly constant. There were no distractions introduced by administrative work, teaching, grading, or even interaction with my colleagues. For better or for worse, all I thought about was my mother, both when I was by her side and when I was a thousand miles away. This extreme level of attention I experienced produced a paradoxical circumstance wherein distance brought me into the presence of my mother, regardless of how physically removed from her I was.

I spent five intense days with my mother and my sisters before flying back home to New York on December 22 to be with my husband and three sons for Christmas. During that time, Mom's condition improved a little bit each day, producing in us a gradually growing hope that she might become strong enough to undergo the surgery to repair her hip, yet she was by no means out of the woods. Thus, we were forced to entertain the opposing emotions of hope and fear at the same time.

I remember the day before my departure most vividly: it was December 21, the pagan feast of the Winter Solstice, a day observed with awe and trepidation by ancient people as the shortest day of the year. Here is another excerpt from my journal, written several days after:

> I spent the Winter Solstice with my sisters and my mother. We sat in her hospital room and looked out the window at the grass, the swaying palm trees, the bright Florida light that transforms all.
>
> We had eaten a beautiful lunch at the Dockside Restaurant seated in the sun. We drank glasses of chilled white wine. Then we returned to her bedside.
>
> "The darkest day of the year," I recalled, in Robert Frost's words. I recited his poem, "Stopping by Woods on a Snowy Evening." (This strangely irritated Rose. My habit of reaching for the words of others to say the unsayable was an annoying trait.)

> Meanwhile our mother lay there in her distant
> pain—full of morphine, breathing heavily, utterly
> alone in her suffering, despite our ready presence.
> A dark day. Its brightness unreal.

The paradox of the winter solstice—the darkest day and, yet, the gateway to the gradual increase of light with each new day—intensified my sense of the paradox of our mother's condition. The solstice is a moment of transition, a narrow threshold over which we must pass in order to reach the season of rebirth. Perhaps our mother was poised at this very transition, preparing to pass out of this old life and burst into a new, fuller one. It also made me feel more acutely the contrast evident in our current circumstance: my sisters and I, as healthy women in the prime of middle age, keeping watch over our mother's damaged body nearing the end of its life. It made me feel fragile, yes, to witness the tyranny of time. But it also made me feel intensely alive. My heart rejoiced in gratitude for the blessing of the light that filled me with joy, the feel of warm sun on my skin, the sight of bright red hibiscus outside the window, the flavors of good food and wine that we were still able to enjoy. Perhaps these sensations were what moved me to recall and recite Frost's poem (another instance of the Sacrament of Speech asserting itself) as a kind of prayer against the darkness, especially its haunting final lines: "The woods are lovely, dark and deep, / but I have promises to keep, / and miles to go before I sleep, / and miles to go before I sleep."[1] We were there to see our mother on her journey into the dark, but we weren't going there—at least not yet.

Praying from a Distance

During the Christmas holiday, my sisters updated me daily on Mom's condition. She was scheduled for surgery on several occasions, but on each of those occasions the doctors changed their minds at the last minute. Finally, on December 28, nearly two weeks after her fall, they said they could wait no longer. The doctors gave her a 70 percent chance of recovery, and my eldest brother had arrived in time to see her before the operation. It was the Feast of the Massacre of the Holy Innocents, a day that did not seem propitious for any undertaking, but liturgical time and hospital time had little to do with one another.

Back in New York, I was snowed in. This was the second in a series of blizzards that would hit the Northeast during that bitter winter of 2009 to 2010, shutting down the nation's busiest airports repeatedly. The cataclysm we were experiencing in the small world of our own lives seemed to be enacted in the stratosphere, over and over again, as if the weather gods were dramatizing on a grand scale our family *agon*. Though I knew better than to believe this, I could not help but *think* it. The proximity of death and disaster somehow heightens the meaning of everything. Prevented from traveling to be with my ailing mother, there seemed to be no practical way I could help, so I did the three things that occurred to me: I lit a candle, I prayed, and I wrote poetry.

At 3:00 p.m., as my mother was wheeled on her gurney through the doors of the operating room, I struck a match and lit the long wick of a novena candle bearing the image of St. Anthony (a synchronicity I can only imagine and hope was true). Novena candles have long been a staple in our house, lined up along the windowsills, placed on every tabletop, standing sentinel on the serpentine wall of the garden. Ever since I had begun working in the Bronx eight years ago and became acquainted with Latin American Catholicism, I had been taken with its fervor. I admired the fierce devotion of the diminutive, elderly women who scrubbed the steps at Our Lady of Mt. Carmel Church on 187th Street—a formerly Italian mission parish that now had more members from South and Central America than from South and Central Italy. I loved the unabashed piety evidenced in the images of Our Lady of Guadalupe hung behind the counters of the neighborhood bodegas, the dollar stores, and even the Rite Aid on Arthur and Crescent Avenues. In fact, I had developed the habit of buying the novena candles whenever—and wherever—I could and using them to light our evening meals, both when dining inside and outside on our patio during the summer months. The symbol of the lone candle in the darkness is such a powerful one—particularly when that flame illuminates the brilliant image of the Blessed Virgin, the Sacred Heart, or some storied saint.

I would choose the saints for a variety of reasons—some were our name saints and some were favorites on account of their charisms. I loved the image of St. Martha leading a dragon on a chain, emblematic of the power of feminine domesticity to tame our primitive drives and, in particular, I loved the image of the Virgin of Guadalupe poised in serene prayer against the rainbow colors of Juan Diego's *tilma*. I bought St. Anthony candles because he was beloved by my mother. As was the case in many an Italian-American household, he was our family's go-to saint. We prayed to him when we had lost things, yes—but he was capable of so much more. St. Anthony could restore a lost love, a peaceful state of mind, a friendship that had been broken, and even one's lost faith.

He was the gentle saint, always depicted holding the baby Jesus, and therefore tender and fatherly in his attention to those who called on him. I wasn't sure how many of these powers were accorded to St. Anthony by Church tradition and how many of them he was granted by my mother, but that hardly mattered. We believed them all.

My mother was a fervent, but not a particularly observant, Catholic. The product of Catholic schooling, she had been taught all of the Articles of Faith as a child, but as an adult she found herself living in defiance of them. Her divorce at age seventeen from her first husband (a marriage hastily and foolishly made) and her subsequent civil marriage placed her firmly outside of the Church. However, this did not stop her from going to Mass; quite the contrary, she would wake us early on Sunday morning, dress the five of us in our best clothes, and march us off to Our Lady of Sorrows Church for the 9:00 Mass, sometimes the 7:30. (Any of the later Masses she referred to as "the lazy man's Mass.") We always sat close to the front (about seven pews back), a practice that made her conspicuous when she did not process to the altar rail for Communion with the rest of us. In all the years we attended church together, I never saw my mother receive the Eucharist. In fact, the first and only time I did see her receive Communion was in the nursing home a few weeks before she died—a sight that moved me beyond words.

Significantly, my father never attended Mass. This was partly due to the customary practice of Italian men at the time. The few who did go usually did so on holidays, and then they stood in the back or even outside on the steps of the church—as if reluctant to participate. The message was clear: with the exception of the priest on the altar and the altar boys, religion was women's work.

The image of my mother at Communion, marooned in the pew, her black mantilla shadowing her dark eyes, is one that haunts me. (Somehow I think here of the single candle burning in the darkness.) There is such power in this witness of faith—the fact that she kept coming back, despite the fact that the Church had rendered her an ex-communicant. She was in the Church, but not of it—no longer part of the Body of Christ—and yet she refused to be excluded. She still went to Mass, prayed, and even sang the hymns in her fine soprano, one of the loudest voices in the church. This was a conundrum for me when I was growing up, but one I confess I enjoyed, for it made her special. Perhaps, in my childish mind, I associated this solitary woman, called out from the rest for a different kind of fate, with other women I had heard about in church who transgressed the boundaries of their religion and culture: Mary Magdalene, the woman taken in adultery, the woman with the flow of blood, the woman who wept, as well as the one who sat at Jesus' feet, the woman at the well, and even the Virgin Mary herself. (The fact that my mother's name was Marion aided me in making such associations, I'm sure—so many of these women were Marys.)

My mother was Catholic from a distance, and that distance seemed to afford her an appreciation of the Church, its prayers, its music, and especially its sacraments, which those who were enveloped in the bosom of the Church often took for granted. I think of Emily Dickinson's poem in which she writes, "Success is counted sweetest / by those who ne'er succeed."[2] Dickinson (another woman who lived on the margins of life) knew that the essence of a thing is most fully appreciated from a distance, by those who desire but do not possess it. In theological terms, this is the *via negativa* experienced by saints and mystics, such as St. John of the Cross, wherein one comes to know a spiritual state by its opposite. There is no better teacher of light than darkness, the saint discovers. Similarly, Dickinson writes, "Water is taught by thirst."[3] Because of this wisdom tradition, I think it very likely that my mother understood goodness, sanctity, and virtue living in her (supposedly) sinful, unsanctified marriage in an intense and visceral way—and perhaps even more fully than our neighbors who lived apparently upright lives.

Being Catholic from a distance also empowered her to doubt. My mother often questioned Church teachings in our hearing. I remember being scandalized when I was a child as I overheard her proclaim with absolute certainty, shortly after our father's untimely death: "There's no such thing as hell. Hell is right here on earth." (I waited for the thunderbolt from heaven—but it never came.) As the years passed and my young, attractive mother began to date other men in the hope of remarrying, it gradually became clear to me that the Church's prohibition of sex outside of marriage meant little to her as well. (I suppose this makes a great deal of sense, since her long and faithful marriage to my father was seen as an adulterous relationship in the Church's eyes. She had been disobeying this rule for a very long time.)

Rebellious and unorthodox as our mother was, she had a hunger for holiness and she found it where she could. One form her reverence took was her devotion to St. Anthony and absolute faith in his powers. In fact, when I think back on our rather unusual practice of prayer, I remember her invoking his name far more often than the name of Jesus, Mary, or God. Perhaps because he had been merely human, like her— imperfect in that humanity—she felt more confident of his sympathy and assistance.

Now, decades later, as my aged and injured mother slipped into the darkness of anesthesia in a Florida operating room, and as I found myself lighting a candle to accompany her from a distance in her struggle for life, it seemed inevitable that the candle should bear the image of her patron saint. This ordinary object, purchased at an ordinary bodega in the Bronx, now served the purpose of a sacramental, a symbol of our common belief in the presence of God in the world, in the mediating power of Christ and all the saints to relieve suffering, and in the continuing operation of grace in her life. It united our past with this present moment and lit our way to the future toward which we were inexorably traveling.

The Sacrament of Poetry

Prayer and poetry both participate in the Sacrament of Speech, albeit in different ways. Prayer can take many forms: the repetition of fixed prayers and prayer formulas (such as the Our Father, the Hail Mary, or the Rosary); the recitation of the Psalms (the Church's most ancient prayers); and the articulation of spontaneous prayer of the heart, among other possibilities. Each of these forms of prayer most often entails speech, the actual *saying* of the words—an activity that involves the body (the lips, teeth, tongue, vocal chords, and lungs) as well as the mind of the praying person. In addition, we often employ particular postures when we pray—the folding or the opening of the hands, the downward casting of the eyes, the fist touching the chest, the getting down upon one's knees. Sacrament engages the body, along with ordinary material reality, in an attempt to transcend the bounds of corporality, time, and space and touch eternity. Through these words and these actions, we acknowledge God's presence in everything, including our frail and mortal bodies, and we dispose our-selves toward the divine grace that pervades all.

The making of poetry, like the action of prayer, also engages the body and material reality. Like those who pray, most poets enact a kind of ritual—often one of their own devising—when they write. The poet usually writes in a particular room, seated at a favorite desk or chair, and often at a carefully appointed time of day. Most poets—even in our technologically advanced era—still write poems in a notebook, one that is carefully chosen for size, feel, and function, and they often use a favorite pen (or kind of pen) to write. Those who use computers typically use one carefully chosen to suit their needs, just as writers of a bygone era had a favorite typewriter, its shape and touch and sound all calibrated to effectively channel the writer's sensibility. These seemingly ordinary objects and materials (ink, paper, pen, chair, desk, machine) take on the qualities of sacramentals as they assist the poet in the sacrament of writing poems.

My own discovery of poetry as a sacramental endeavor has unfolded gradually over the years. As my siblings would attest, I was a talker from an early age and loved the sound of words. When I learned to read and write, I also discovered that I had facility with the written word in addition to the spoken, and it wasn't long before I figured out that through the use of rhythm and rhyme, as well as assonance, consonance, and alliteration, I could make words sing. I began composing poems in the first grade, carrying a portfolio of poems (really a manila folder) around with me wherever I went. (How strange—yet somehow comforting—it is to pause here and acknowledge that I am still doing this decades later.)

Writing was not so much a choice as a compulsion. I loved doing it, so I did it. Like any other sort of spontaneous play, writing poetry needed no end beyond itself. Poetry seemed to be something I could manage on my own. All I needed was a pen, some paper, and a ritual. And so I would make music with words.

Years later, as an adult pursuing the twin vocations of poetry and scholarship, I began to discover the long and hallowed tradition associating the creation of art with sacramental activity. Many writers have assisted me in making this connection. To write poetry, Catholic poet Denise Levertov notes, is to labor in the service of the transcendent.[4] Every writer, whether consciously religious or not, gestures by means of the concrete toward the invisible reality that lies all around us in attempt to link time and eternity, the many and the One. This linking, writes poet David Jones, is radically "religious" in nature, since the root meaning of the word "religion" means "to link" or "to bind." Human beings are the only animals who create "gratuitous" works—art that serves no apparent purpose or, alternately, serves some mysterious purpose beyond the practical or the obvious, a purpose that is often unknown to even the artist. In this way, the artist participates in the ongoing action of gratuitous divine creation.[5]

The first act in Judeo-Christian cosmic history is the creation of the universe, as recorded in the book of Genesis. The scriptures do not say *why* God created the heavens and the earth; presumably, they were their own reasons for being. Church teaching suggests that the goodness of creation is the result of the spontaneous overflow of the Creator's immeasurable love. The same can be said of art and of the human beings who make it, attesting to one of the many ways in which man is made in God's image.

Connections such as these helped me to understand why writing had long seemed to me to be a holy activity that shared a kinship with prayer and with sacrament. In Marilynne Robinson's beautiful novel *Gilead*, the main character says, "Writing has always felt to me like praying. You feel like you are *with* someone."[6] Paradoxically, writing—that most solitary of activities—is radically communal.

Given this history of both my heart and my art, it is perhaps no surprise that my accompaniment of my mother from a distance, as she underwent surgery on December 28 and as she endured a rocky recovery over the next several weeks, took the form of almost compulsive writing. From the time of her surgery until I saw her again after her recovery in the nursing home on January 13, I wrote and revised twenty-five new poems. Fourteen of these were sonnets—part of a crown of sonnets, in fact, a complicated pattern of poems in which each subsequent sonnet in the series begins with the concluding line of the previous sonnet. The fourteenth sonnet closes the sequence where it began, thus weaving all of the lines into the shape of a circular "crown."

I confess that the crown of sonnets, titled "A Blessing for My Mother," took me by surprise, for I had never written such a formally demanding poem before, and I did not intend to write one on this occasion. Yet somehow I could not stop myself. I did set out to write the first sonnet—but then, when I arrived at the fourteenth line, I realized I had much more to say, so I simply started the next sonnet using the last line of the previous one. Working in this way—slowly and painstakingly—felt like a kind of journey, as if I were making my way across a rapidly running river, each sonnet being a stone upon which I could set my foot, but only momentarily, until it was time to move on. In addition, the journey seemed a perilous one—each first line I threw out (each foot I extended toward the next stone) constituted an act of faith, the belief that there would be a stone to land on.

The content of the poem, in addition to the form, also took me on a kind of journey. The first sonnet began in the present, but as I wrote each subsequent poem, I found myself moving back into the past, stopping to narrate key events in my mother's life and in the life of our family. The sequence, with its fourteen stopping points along the way, gradually took on the feel of a religious procession, as if I were engaged in our family's version of the Stations of the Cross, visiting some of the most painful moments of our life together. All of this felt like sacrament to me: making the ritual round of memory; observing the strict rules of the sonnet form (line length, metrical pattern, rhyme scheme), all of which involve repetition; being constantly attentive to sacramentals (my notebook, my pen, my St. Anthony candle); and, perhaps most important of all, profoundly sensing this activity as a sign and symbol of my love for my mother and my presence to her across a very great distance.

Robert Frost once famously observed that when one suffers any sense of confusion in life, the best thing one can do is create order out of chaos by creating form.[7] I learned the wisdom of this during these hours, days, and weeks. The linguistic forms I engaged in making helped me to focus, to feel less confused and uncertain, and most of all—since I was *doing* something—to feel less helpless. I had no control over my mother's sickness or surgery or inevitable mortality, but *here* was something over which I could exercise some measure of control.

In the face of sickness and death, I was *making* something, deliberately countering the spirit of destruction and desolation in the universe with that of creation and consolation.

Writing poetry became a means of redemption and a way of forgiving myself for my distance from my mother (in the long and in the short term, as well as in the emotional and in the geographic sense), of redeeming our troubled family life, and of healing our fraught relationship. In fact, these poems continue to function, for me, as a redemptive act: each time I reread the sequence, I feel the power of those efficacious words anew. In addition, the poems function in a similar way for readers who encounter them—or so I have been told. Though the details of other lives might vary, the universal condition of families is the same, at its core. We all share the condition of brokenness, though it may take many forms, and we all share the desire for the wholeness we have lost.

The first poem in the sonnet sequence begins and ends as I was taking leave of my mother on December 22 to board my flight back to New York for Christmas. I wet my finger on my tongue and made the Sign of the Cross on her forehead. Lacking chrism or holy water, I made do with what I had, my own saliva, believing Church teaching—as well as the words of poet William Blake—that "everything that lives is holy."[8] This is what transpired in her hospital room:

> Today I spit into my hand and blessed
> my mother. Traced a salivary cross
> upon her dry brow. It caught the winter
> light like chrism on an infant's new skin.
> Bliss of my mother's touch, my origin—
> this grief a lost daughter's only gesture.
> I've unlearned how to love that dear body,
> the arms that held us and the lips that kissed,
> showed us all how to love all that's lovely.
> I've taught my heart the ways she won't be missed,

though I know such delusions just delay
the truth I hear my traitor tongue say,
Forgive the faithless daughter I have been,
as I bless my blesséd mother yet again.[9]

And then I left for home. After a few days of proximity to her, I found myself having to practice the Sacrament of Distance once again.

Chapter 3

THE SACRAMENT OF BEAUTY

Late have I loved you,
Beauty so old and so new.
Late have I loved you.

—St. Augustine

These celebrated words of St. Augustine constitute a poem and a prayer of thanksgiving. In his *Confessions*, Augustine discovers that even in the period of his life when he believed himself to be avoiding God, he was actually pursuing him. Augustine's passion for the things of this world was motivated by his love of their beauty. Without his knowing it, beauty was a means through which God lured and led him toward the Good. Ultimately, the saint's conversion came about as a consequence of this love of beauty.

In his powerful book *Beauty: The Invisible Embrace*, philosopher, priest, and poet John O'Donohue reminds his readers of the urgency with which beauty interrupts ordinary life:

In Greek, the word for "the beautiful" is *to kalon*. It is related to the word *kalein* which includes the notion of "call." When we experience beauty, we feel called. The Beautiful stirs passion and urgency in us and calls us forth from aloneness into the warmth and wonder of an eternal embrace. It unites us again with the neglected and forgotten grandeur of life. Beauty calls to all of us, and does so at odd and unexpected moments. Speaking in whispers and glimpses, it makes itself known to us at the best and the worst times of our lives, and then it inevitably fades, leaving an aura behind it. Beauty visits—it does not linger—but for the few moments it is present to us, we feel renewed, refreshed, transformed. It is a visitation of grace.[1]

One of the epiphanies that came to me during my mother's illness was the discovery of the degree to which her life had been predicated upon the call of beauty. She pursued beauty in its many forms as eagerly as St. Augustine did—desiring and acquiring beautiful clothes, cultivating her own personal beauty, falling in love with handsome men; even her move to Florida, late in life, was the result of her having visited and fallen in love with its palm trees, its blue sea and sky, and its dramatic sunsets.

I simultaneously became aware of the fact that the pattern of my own life, as well as those of my sisters, had been shaped by the pursuit of beauty, too, though we heard its call in other ways. This commonality that we shared, despite our many differences, became a *lingua franca* for us during the final days of my mother's life. We would cultivate beauty, practice it as the sacrament it is, and embody it in our speech and gestures and in our handling of ordinary material objects. We all understood, tacitly, that beauty was a good, redeeming presence in our lives both past and present, and that we would do all we could to invite and pursue it, even—and especially—in the face of imminent death.

Kairos: Time Redeemed and Beautified

In tragedy, there is often a moment in the play or film shortly before the final disaster when the audience is deluded into hoping for a happy ending. This moment—wherein we hope Juliet might awaken from her feigned death before Romeo takes his life, that Hamlet might finally take his revenge upon his murderous uncle and live to tell the tale, that Michael Corleone might outwit his enemies and save his family and himself from a violent end—is a "false dawn." The dramatist provides just a hint of light on the dark horizon, and the audience almost believes it to be the rising sun; however, we also know in our hearts that it is not. So powerful is our desire for this happy ending that we sometimes find ourselves rooting for it even though we have seen the play before and we know exactly how it must end.

The seemingly successful surgery performed on our mother and her brief recovery afterward proved to be a false dawn for us. The difference was that this was real life, *our* life, rather than the imagined lives of characters on the stage and screen. I long ago learned that art imitates and, in some ways, prepares us for life—but somehow a lifetime of reading literature and experiencing hope and disappointment vicariously does not spare us the inevitable pain these powerful emotions cause. There is no inoculation against grief.

My mother did eventually die from her initial injury—but, strange as it seems, I am grateful for the extended false dawn our family experienced between her surgery and her final, precipitous decline. For a period of nearly three weeks, our mother progressed from a state of unconsciousness and dependence on a ventilator to one of full awareness, independence from life support, and engagement with the world immediately around her. The mere husk of a woman I encountered when I first saw her in the ICU returned almost miraculously to her former self. More accurately, the Marion who came out of surgery seemed to me to be an earlier version of our mother—before alcohol had altered her personality and robbed her of the pleasures of everyday life.

I was fortunate to visit her for six days during this remarkable transformation, a period that was all too brief but that became for me and my sisters a graced time. It was a form of *kairos*—time that is not measured by the calendar or clock but stands, instead, as a still moment outside of *chronos* and its endless succession of sequential time. As opposed to *chronos*, often portrayed in poetry and art as an ugly devourer of human life, *kairos* is portrayed as a beautiful child, full of potential and possibility. *Kairos* implies cessation, a brief reprieve from the demands of the tyrant time. This stillness—or, as writer Andre Dubus terms it in his essay, "On Charon's Wharf," this "pause in the March" toward mortality that we all engage in—offered us the extraordinary and unexpected opportunity to redeem past actions and set a new course for the future.[2]

In the course of six days, we three sisters received a great gift: occasion upon occasion to demonstrate our love for our mother, affirm our relationship to her as mother and daughters, and heal some of the deep wounds that had marred our family life for decades. Six days may not seem like a lot of time, and there is a part of me that wishes our *kairos* had been longer. But another part of me knows that six days is sufficient time to accomplish a great deal—to create a new universe, in fact, as Genesis reminds us. And that is, in some ways, what we were able to do.

THE SHOCK OF RECOGNITION

When I arrived at the Indian River Nursing Home on January 13, my sister Charlene led me down a long, bright corridor, cheerfully chattering about Mom's anticipation of my visit. Charlene described the colorful sign she had made and propped on my mother's food tray as a daily reminder of something to look forward to. (It moved me very much to see that sign when I ultimately entered the room: "Angela is coming soon!" I thought of the Benedictines and their hospitality, the directive to receive all guests as if they were Christ.) She also told me Mom had requested that she be dressed in her new robe and even asked to wear her wig in honor of the occasion. (Wigs and hairpieces had long been part of Mom's "big hair" aesthetic, an attempt to augment her less-than-abundant black hair.) Always attractive and always preoccupied with her appearance, Mom wanted to look her best for my arrival.

The hallway was lined with old people seated in wheelchairs. Many of them were slumped down in various states of near or total unconsciousness; a very few were erect and alert enough to show interest in our passing and follow us with their eyes. I remember one white-haired, blue-eyed woman in particular, who smiled sweetly as I passed. I looked at each face, expecting at any moment to encounter my mother's— and then I saw the signature black wig on a woman whose back was turned to us. The familiarity of her outline and posture sent a surge of joy through me—to see her upright after having seen her entirely prostrate just weeks before—but as I rushed round the front of the wheelchair to greet her, I stopped dead. The woman who looked up at me was a complete stranger—her small black eyes appeared unnaturally bright and nervous, and there was no hint of recognition in them. Thin as she was, her facial features were extremely pronounced: the nose seemed a comically exaggerated version of my mother's noble Roman nose, the brow prominent and stern, and the mouth wizened and shapeless since it lacked teeth to give it defini-tion. This poor woman, who was obviously in a state of acute anxiety, gave the impression of a bright-eyed bird of prey. She looked mildly insane.

I was stunned at first by this apparition and then imme-diately relieved, for I was certain that this woman was not my mother. A terrible mistake had been made, and I'm ashamed to admit that I was grateful not to have to claim her as kin. But my sister confirmed what I had hoped was not true, be-cause she said to this woman, with her characteristic enthusi-asm, "Look, Mom! I told you Angela was coming—and here she is!"

It's difficult to describe in any orderly way the chaos of conflicting emotions that accompanied this shock of recogni-tion. My mother's face remained emotionless—a hard, impas-sive mask—as I dutifully bent down to hug her and to kiss her cheek. And I wondered if this was her response to my obvious confusion, alarm, relief, and renewed horror upon discover-ing who she was or whether she was as mentally confused as her appearance suggested. I felt guilty, as though I had be-trayed her in some way by not knowing her. But, in truth, she seemed to have become someone else. My beautiful mother was no longer beautiful and would never be beautiful again.

Looking back on this moment (which still pains me when-ever I recall it), I sometimes wonder whether my seeming inability to recognize her was, in reality, a refusal to admit the beginning of my loss of her, and ultimately the inevitable loss of myself. I don't believe I can ever fully understand my motivations or articulate the revelations that came to me in those few seconds of time. But I do believe that moment was significant in ways that will continue to reveal themselves to me as long as my memory retains the image of her terribly altered face.

THE PURSUIT OF BEAUTY

One of the many ways in which I misunderstood my mother, in the course of our lives together, was my mistaking her lifelong preoccupation with her appearance for simple vanity. My mother was part of a generation of women who had been conditioned by American culture to consider their worth as human beings to be commensurate with their physical attractiveness and measured by the attention they received from admiring men. During the years of her childhood and young adulthood, female film stars such as Marilyn Monroe and Elizabeth Taylor established the norms for female beauty, and many women tried to achieve these standards by emulating the makeup, hairstyles, dress, and demeanor of their idols. (Because she was dark-haired and dark-eyed, my mother's particular models were Taylor and Sophia Loren. In fact, she identified with the former so thoroughly that when Elizabeth Taylor died about a year after my mother did, I grieved as if I were losing her all over again.)

This behavior was not a part of the culture of my childhood. The economic and political strides made by the women's movement of the 1960s and 1970s offered girls and women in subsequent generations choices and alternative ways of distinguishing themselves that were not widely available to women of my mother's era. No longer confined to using their sexuality as the sole means of empowerment, women began to steer the course of their own lives by developing their intellectual capabilities through education and claiming economic freedom by taking jobs and preparing for professions that had previously been open only to men. As a child of this new dispensation, I relished going to school, enjoyed the challenge of academic endeavor, and excelled as a student.

My mother's response to my success in school was less than enthusiastic. For one thing, it established a division between us, yet another form of distance separating us. As she confessed to me, years later, she felt it strange that she never needed to help me with what she termed "your lessons." Looking back on incidents in my childhood, it seems at times that my intelligence was a threat and an affront. One day after school when I was in the third or fourth grade, I came home excitedly to report to my mother that I had earned straight one hundreds on my report card. My mother greeted this news with an uncomfortable silence. She didn't even glance up from her task but, instead, continued working at the kitchen stove, carefully scouring the white porcelain top. After a few seconds (though it seems much longer in my memory), she broke the silence. "Angela, 'He that is exalted shall be humbled, and he that is humbled shall be exalted.'"

I was floored by this response. First, I was struck by how little stock she put in the academic accomplishments so many other parents actively tried to cultivate in their children. Second, I had no idea where she had heard such elevated language. This was not my mother's typical idiom, and I knew it. Though I never solved the first conundrum, within an hour I was able to understand the second. I happened to glance at the calendar that hung on our kitchen wall—it was a Catholic calendar, a free gift given out at our parish church every January, and each day of the month listed any Church holidays, the liturgical season, saints' feast days, and finally a scripture passage for the day. My eye lit on the date, and there I saw the passage from the twenty-third chapter of Matthew that my mother had just quoted to me (without attribution, I might add).

I still remember the strange commingling of sorrow and delight I felt at discovering this. If this was a game of cat and mouse, I was definitely winning. But this was small consolation, for I never wanted to play the game in the first place.

Among my siblings I had earned a reputation as "the smart kid" (deserved or not), and perhaps I enjoyed this distinction more than I ought to have. This might account for another of my mother's characteristic attitudes toward me. From my childhood through my young adulthood, whenever there was public knowledge in my family of a mistake I had made—buying the wrong item at the store or losing a valued possession—my mother would inevitably intone, "For such an intelligent person, Angela, you certainly are stupid!" I felt its sting—but not because I believed what she said was true. I somehow knew her insult came from her own insecurity and distaste that she had developed toward me.

At the time, I did not understand the degree to which this mother-daughter conflict was grounded in our generational difference. But I've come to recognize it as operative in our relationship almost from the very start. This is not to say I did not value my mother. When I was a child, I was proud of my mother's beauty—proud of the fact that when she came to school to visit, she wore a dress and high heels, rather than the dowdy housecoat and the clumsy work shoes so many of the

other mothers would wear. Ours was a blue-collar community, and many of these mothers were beset by too much work
and too many children to lavish attention on themselves. Our
mother, by contrast, seemed self-confident, elegant, and sophisticated, despite her five children, her ailing husband, and
the fact that she worked hard both in and outside the home.
She would never dream of leaving the house wearing stock-
ings with holes in them or going to the market without first
putting on lipstick and makeup. (Unlike the woman in the
wheelchair at the nursing home, *this* was the mother I had
been proud to claim.)

However, as I grew older, I came to regard my mother's
preoccupation with her appearance—and the appearance of
others—as a sign of her shallowness. I didn't like her brutal as-
sessments of others, especially of other women. I also resented
her evident disapproval of me—not only because I was "too
smart for my own good" (her phrase), but because I was not
as feminine, as conventionally attractive, or as interested in
my own beauty. As I grew older, I dressed as I pleased, and she
was clearly unhappy when I gave up wearing makeup during
college. My standards and my tastes were not my mother's,
and she sent signals, in a thousand different ways, to let me
know that she disapproved of me. To further add to this division between us, my older sisters did conform more closely
to my mother's ideas about feminine dress and behavior. As
a result, the three of them seemed to be part of a "girls' club"
from which I had been involuntarily exiled.

It is only in recent years that I have been able to understand my mother's obsession with this limited form of beauty
differently, more charitably, and (I hope) more wisely. In some
ways, her perspective was practically inevitable because of the
time and circumstances of her formation as a woman, and

it seemed to also be a sign of her desire to achieve a kind of elusive perfection.

In my own life, I was fortunate to discover learning and, ultimately, writing as a means to the beauty I desired—just as in the lives of singers music becomes the means to that end, and in the lives of artists painting or sculpting stone becomes their obsession. In fact, I believe that at some level my mother possessed an artistic temperament, along with an innate love of beauty, but that she had not been encouraged or trained to seek or express that beauty beyond the conventional cultivation of feminine attractiveness. Indeed, as a child she had taken tap-dance lessons as well as singing lessons, and these made her happy. (One of our family's prized possessions is a professional studio portrait of our mother at age ten wearing her tap shoes and dance outfit. The camera seems to have caught her just as she finished her routine with a flourish, her hands extended at her side in a gesture of victory. "Here I am, world!" she seems to be saying, an announcement made emphatic by her confident eyes and beautiful smile.) My mother kept her tap shoes well into old age. Eventually, family circumstances forced her to give up both dancing and singing. The void left behind had to be filled in some way—and so it was.

I narrate this history in an effort to demonstrate the degree to which the concept of beauty was a painful subject and a cause for separation between us rather than a source of unity, as it is for many mothers and daughters. It also highlights how strange and poignant a fact it is that at the end of her life, during the six days of our *kairos* time together, our love of beauty in its various forms became a source of consolation. The very quality in her I had long disliked gradually had become, for me, a sign of a passion we held in common, and a relationship broken by beauty was about to be repaired by it.

BEAUTY IN THE SICK ROOM

After the initial disaster of our reunion, the first day of my visit with my mother went remarkably well, as did the five days that followed. Though my sisters and I never consciously stated this, the goal we had in common was to make our mother as comfortable as possible and also to try to restore a sense of normality. Mom always enjoyed being the center of attention—one of her favorite expressions was "I'm the important person here!"—and though this selfish quality in her had driven us crazy for many years, we were more than happy to oblige her in these particular circumstances. This might explain why a restoration of her sense of beauty—both her own and beauty in the space around her—became an unspoken priority for us.

It may seem pathetic, from some perspectives, that an old woman just returned from death's door would care about whether she looked pretty, but I found this deeply poignant. I remember one moment in particular that struck me powerfully. An hour after my arrival, one of the doctors caring for my mother stopped by the room to check on her. She was a beautiful, young Indian woman named Anna, a name very close to my own. Anna had thick, black hair; smooth, coffee-colored skin; and brilliant, black eyes. Most arresting of all was her smile, which lit up her face and the drab sick room around her. As she stepped into the room, greeted us, and began speaking with me and my sister Charlene, my mother looked sheepishly up from her wheelchair, interrupted us, and announced loudly: "Look at the three of you! You're all so beautiful. And look at me—I'm a mess!"

Startled, we all paused and, for the first time, attentively looked at one another. I was wearing my sleeveless black dress, my best leather boots, a black beret, and a long, red scarf. My sister was wearing a black skirt, sling-back heels, and a striped white jacket. Dr. Anna wore a hospital-issued white coat, but such was her beauty that she looked lovely in everything. I suddenly realized that my mother was right—given the freedom and time to prepare ourselves to encounter the world, we each looked our best, while she, ruined by her poor health and marooned in her wheelchair, looked her worst. Since she had been used to a lifetime of being one of the most attractive women in any room she entered, how painful it must have been for her to recognize that this was no longer so.

This incident set her, and us, on a quest to return her to her former self—or, at least, toward some semblance of that. The processes we would engage in during the next few days had a practical end, in some ways. Helping Mom to feel better about herself and the space around her would encourage hope and nurture her resolve to recover and her will to live. But I realized, even as we were enacting these beauty rituals, that their primary goal was spiritual in nature. We wanted to nourish and nurture our mother's love of beauty, the one virtue that was powerful enough to pull her out of herself, take her beyond the realm of suffering, and enable her to set her eyes and her heart on the possibility of joy. Just as I am convinced of my mother's artistic temperament, I am also convinced that beauty was the means through which our mother most readily apprehended God. Beauty is a conduit of grace, and the absence of the one in her immediate circumstance seemed to imply the absence of the other.

Many saints and holy people have acknowledged the role of beauty in leading them to God. In the opening of this chapter, St. Augustine offers a justly famous paean to the transient earthly beauty of creation as an incarnation of the eternal beauty of the divine. This flawed saint's relentless appetite for the beautiful led him, ultimately, to God.

If this can be true of the Bishop of Hippo, then why not my mother? I reasoned. Surely she was no more sinful than he, and surely God loves her no less. As for the seeming folly of finding beauty in the sick room, *If not here, where?* I wondered. The sick room is, in a sense, the suffering world in small, and we all need beauty, even—and perhaps especially—in the face of death.

THE VOCATION OF BEAUTY

Just as I have discovered in recent years that the love of beauty was common ground that my mother and I shared, I have also come to discover that my sisters share it as well. All three of us practice professions and vocations that enable us to bring beauty into the lives of others. My oldest sister, Rose Ann, attended cosmetology school as a young woman—not so much by choice as by my mother's insistence, since that seemed a profession she could master quickly and, thereafter, derive a steady income. (Immediately after our father's death, we children had to help my mother hold the household together, financially and otherwise, so attending college and taking time to choose one's own profession was a luxury unavailable to my older siblings.)

Happily, my sister excelled at her work and also proved to have an excellent head for business, enabling her to start her own salon and earn a very good living at her profession from an early age. My sister has been working with some of her clients for decades, helping these women, as they slowly age and lose their youthful, natural beauty, to compensate for that loss and to discover in their changing faces and hair colors and textures a new version of themselves—one they can live with happily and confidently. I have seen women enter my sister's salon looking depleted and worn and then leave afterward seemingly revived, restored, and ready to do battle with whatever difficulties life may send their way. I have also seen her turn an ordinary-looking young woman into a spectacularly beautiful bride, filling her wedding day with joy for her and for all who beheld her.

My second sister (our middle sister), Charlene, has an eye for beauty along with clever hands that enable her to practice it. Having married a painting contractor at a young age, she and her husband founded a business together, and among her many roles (including decorating consultant and business manager), she became highly skilled at the art of hanging wallpaper. Charlene delights in color and design and is able to provide expert advice (as well as execute the practical labor) that turns an ordinary room into a beautiful living space. She has transformed many spaces in the homes of people all over south and central Florida, making thousands of people happy and grateful for the contact with beauty they enjoy on a daily basis.

As for me, my pursuit of beauty has long taken the form of reading literature and writing poetry, but I have loved the arts in their many forms. Nothing delights me more than going to museums to see the work of an artist's imagination represented through paint and stone, going to concerts to hear good music performed by gifted artists, attending plays brought to life through the voices and bodies of fine actors, and watching movies created and orchestrated by visionary filmmakers. These experiences of beauty make me feel intensely present in the moment and more fully *alive*. I feel as if I am in the immediate presence of the creative genius who created the object I am beholding and also, by extension, of the God who has authored all the beauty in the world from the beginning of time to the present. In addition, I am blessed to work in a profession that engages my vocation. As a literature professor, I earn my daily bread by offering works of great beauty to my students for their consideration in an attempt to engender in them the same love and appreciation that my mentors once engendered in me. Thus, observing, making, and sharing beauty is my way of being in the world, just as it is for my sisters and was for my mother as well, after a fashion.

THE PRACTICE OF BEAUTY

When my sister Rose Ann arrived at the nursing home a few hours after my arrival, my mother let her know that she was late. All afternoon Mom had complained about the fact that her hair was a mess and that she needed a manicure badly, and her expectation was that as soon as my cosmetologist sister arrived, she would take care of these needs. My sister rose to the occasion—much as she had throughout the many years she had been practicing her craft on our mother. Moments after she entered the room, she took out her scissors (a tool she never travels without) and asked Mom what hairstyle she wanted. Though Mom had been vociferous about wanting a haircut, her high level of anxiety and also the lingering pain she was feeling in her hip didn't permit her to think clearly or articulate what specific style she wanted. At that point, I suggested a bob—something short, youthful, and playful to give her a jaunty air and to militate against the deadly serious atmosphere of the nursing home.

Rose immediately went to work and cut her hair expertly. As the hair fell past her shoulders onto the floor, a new outline of my mother took shape. Gradually, she lost resemblance to the crazed woman wearing the too-big wig I had seen a few hours before. Instead, her features were softened; her hair, now tamed, framed her face rather than overwhelmed it; and it struck me, as I watched this transformation, that I had never seen her look quite as chic as she did in this simple haircut. She reminded me of women of the flapper era, defiant of traditional modes of beauty with their startling, new, masculine hairstyles. It made me see her, at this advanced stage of our relationship, in a whole new light.

One of the primary ideas that characterizes Catholic theology is the intense emphasis on incarnation as the medium of our lives—as fleshly creatures living in a material world—and as a powerful informing influence on our relationships. The ways in which we hear, see, touch, and experience one another shape and determine our understanding of the mystery of the other as well as of the mystery of our own complex self. Physicality is inextricably tied up with our spiritual being, and through our senses—those doors of perception—we get glimpses of the invisible and eternal I AM that animates us all. These may seem heady thoughts to emerge in response to a haircut, but these are the thoughts that entered and stayed in my mind as I beheld my mother and the remarkable fact that, even after nearly fifty years of knowing her, there were still hidden mysteries being revealed to me.

Mom seemed pleased as we all admired her new haircut, and I was grateful to my sister for her skill and the ease with which she was able to quell Mom's anxiety about her appearance. I was also moved as she took on the task of carefully filing, trimming, and painting our mother's fingernails and toenails. As I watched her put Mom's hand in her lap, gently reposition each of her swollen feet, and deliberately apply the brightly colored polish to all twenty of her nails, it struck me that the act of touching the body of a sick person in an effort to ameliorate her condition spoke powerfully of love and solidarity.

These simple actions assured my mother that she was loved, that we were there for her, and that no harm would befall her while we were there to stave it off. For the sake of completeness and truth, though, I have to confess that a few hours later, when Mom actually looked in the mirror, she was not happy with what she saw. In fact, she was distressed at the haircut "we" had given her, claiming it was too short and made her look ugly, and she would remind us of this failure to please often in the days to come. But this did not bother us since we were accustomed to her complaining about our handiwork, and her dissatisfaction did nothing to diminish her stylish new look. Whether Mom appreciated the Sacrament of Beauty my sister had administered or not, it was efficacious in important ways, and the lift it gave her spirit was obvious, even in the energy of her disapproval. The old Marion was back.

On the second day of my visit, we addressed the next challenge in the makeover we seemed to (inadvertently) be giving my mother—her wardrobe. Mom had been brought from the hospital, so she had nothing to wear besides the hospital gowns (the kind that tied in the back) and the nice, new robe Charlene had bought her for her stay. Accordingly, en route to the nursing home the next day, we stopped at a local discount clothing store that happened to be on the way to choose some new outfits. Looking back on that day and the way my sister and I breezed up and down the aisles of the shop, pulling jumpers, cotton shells, flowered dresses, and colorful warm-up suits off the racks and loading them into our carts, it seems we might have been shopping for our young daughters rather than our ancient mother. It was such a hopeful gesture—gathering these gifts, hoping she might like them, anticipating her delight when we arrived at her sober room with shopping bags full of crisp, new clothes for her to try on. The sheer amount of stuff we bought attests to the measure of our hope—clearly we thought she would be with us for a long time. In retrospect, this might be seen as folly, but I prefer to see it as an act of faith.

It is an old piece of wisdom that when one begins a new endeavor, one ought to put on new clothes. The clothing we choose to wear is one of the many ways we communicate without words. Wearing one's best suit to a wedding or a funeral is a sign of our respect. Dressing meticulously for a job interview signals to our potential employer that we intend to do meticulous work—to both do and look our best—should we be invited to be part of their company. I have heard elementary-school teachers attest repeatedly that their favorite day of the year is picture day—the day their young charges show up to school wearing dresses and ties, sport coats and shiny shoes—because these typically unruly and inattentive children show up transformed into thoughtful young women and young men. They are more serious, more focused, more respectful of one another, and eminently more teachable. On picture day, teachers get a glimpse of the adults the children in their charge will become.

In keeping with its strong incarnational bent, the Catholic Church takes seriously the sacramental significance of clothes. The priest must wear his stole when he carries out his priestly duties—baptizing, hearing Confession, consecrating Eucharist, performing a wedding ceremony, and giving Last Rites. The monk wears a scapular of a particular kind, indicative of his order, and lay persons may wear smaller versions of these as a demonstration of their devotion to a particular order or saint. The bishop carries his crosier—a version of the crook the shepherd uses to drive his sheep—indicative of his pastoral office and the care he exercises for his flock. The baby is baptized in white, indicative of purity and innocence, and a white garment is placed upon her as she receives the sacrament, symbolic of her new life in Christ. Similarly, a white cloth is laid upon the coffin of the deceased at his funeral. It echoes the garment received at Baptism, closing the circle of symbols, even as the departed is ushered into the final step in his lifelong journey toward God.

The color and kinds of clothes one wears also correspond to the seasons of the year in addition to the sacramental moments in life. The entire liturgical year is characterized by different-colored garments that the priest wears: purple for Advent and Lent; white for Christmastide and Easter; red for Palm Sunday, Good Friday, and martyrs' feast days; and green for ordinary time. None of this is left to accident or chance since clothing aids and assists us in celebrating the sacraments and observing the important moments in the Church year.

Knowing all of this, how could we not take seriously the task of arraying our mother for what would be her final days? Much to our delight, our mother loved the clothes we brought her. I pulled each outfit out of its bag, placed it against my body, conducting a mock fashion show, and then handed it to my sister Charlene, who neatly hung each item up in the demi-closet in my mother's room. We asked her which one she wanted to wear first, and she chose a short, black jumper with a white, cotton top.

After we helped her to put it on—more accurately, after we dressed her, much as one would dress a child—we marveled at how good it looked on her. I even took pictures on my cell phone to allow her to see how she looked. I remember these few hours with particular fondness. They constitute a ritual every woman will recognize—the shopping and the homecoming, followed by the fashion show and the simple delight one inevitably takes in a lovely new object to call one's own. It's a celebration of beauty that is often maligned and trivialized by intellectuals and cultural critics (the professional world wherein I spend much of my life).

But such a vision is partial and denies a basic human pleasure that is real and life affirming. The clothes a person arrays one's body with do *matter*, just as surely as the body beneath does. I see the three of us in that room practicing the Sacrament of Beauty—giving and receiving while united in a common purpose—and feeling the force of gratitude and grace, knowing we are in the presence of love and therefore God. And all of this was on account of a few new clothes.

The Sacrament of Naming

The challenge of creating beautiful surroundings in my mother's sickroom proved to be more difficult than that of beautifying her body, but we did our best. Both of my sisters and I had brought in framed photographs of our family to arrange around the room. Mom enjoyed looking at the pictures of her grandchildren, of our individual families, and of all of us together, which had been taken at celebratory occasions. The latter, in particular, held her interest, since she would look at each face, name each person, and then remark on how beautiful or handsome he or she looked. This exercise served a practical purpose, to aid her failing memory, and also a spiritual one—to remind her that many people loved her and, even though they could not be present, they were thinking of and praying for her.

These photographs took up a good deal of surface space in the room, but most of the hospital staff seemed not to mind, with several showing an interest in the people in the pictures, remarking on them and asking questions about their identities. This, however, was not the case with everyone. Three days after my arrival, a night nurse came in and became agitated over the photos, so much so that she began picking them up off the counter, tray, and shelving, stacking them on top of one another noisily, and handing them to me. "I've been working here eleven years," she clucked, "and I know what happens to things such as this. They fall on the floor, the glass breaks and goes everywhere, and I have to clean it up. Put 'em away!"

I was too stunned to respond to her unkindness and disrespect other than to dutifully place the pictures in some bags I had in the room where they would be out of the woman's (and my mother's) sight. Truth be told, Mom, in her state of pain, anxiety, and inattentiveness, seemed not to notice when they were missing. But the following evening, when that nurse did not return—and instead a kindly, young, male nurse came on duty—I took them back out of the bags and put them around the room again. My mother seemed delighted to see them (almost as if she had not seen them before), and we resumed the ritual practice of taking them in hand, identifying her loved ones, and remarking on their appearance. This Sacrament of Naming restored calm to my agitated mother, enabling her to focus on something beyond her own pain and predicament. I would not have anticipated that an object as ordinary as a photograph would provide such a healing balm.

THE RITUAL OF READING

Another ritual my mother enjoyed was one we referred to as the "Reading of the Cards." Mom received a number of get-well cards from family members and friends, and we arranged them around the room and on her tray so she might see and be cheered by them. Early on, in one of her difficult moments—when Mom's painkiller had worn off and she had to wait half an hour for another dose—I tried to distract her by reading each of the cards, showing her the pictures, and reading the names of each sender. This proved a delightful distraction and seemed to diminish her pain as well as her anxiety. Some of the cards were humorous, and it struck me as both sad and sweet that she would laugh at the same joke each time I read it as if she hadn't heard it before. I also felt a pang at the role reversal that was becoming familiar ritual by now—I was reading to my mother as I once did to my children, and she seemed glad and willing to assume this new role of childlike dependency.

THE SACRAMENT OF *DIRTY DANCING*

Our efforts to lift my mother's spirits through these accidental rituals brought joy, in glimpses. ("Beauty visits—it does not linger," as John O'Donohue reminds us.) Despite our hopes that our mother would recover, her health was not improving. The surgeons successfully replaced her broken hip, but ahead lay a long road of difficult and painful physical therapy.

My mother had never been a very good patient, and I suspect her pain threshold was not very high. Ten years ago, when she was much stronger, she underwent hip replacement and found the therapy afterward pure agony—so much so that the therapists on staff at the hospital (who are generally patient people) took the unusual step of sending her home and letting her do her exercises with a privately hired, in-home therapist. Such a step was not possible now. Our mother was wheelchair bound—completely unable to care for herself in the most basic ways—and she needed to try to recover the strength and stamina to do the therapy. But she seemed to have no will for the task. Her efforts at physical therapy were feeble at best. During one particular session, we watched helplessly as the therapist assisted her in walking with her walker and our mother cried, "Help me, help me, help me!" piteously during the three minutes it took them to get around the room.

Though there were no major setbacks during this *kairos* period, each day brought a new struggle, a new symptom, and a quiet sign that she was not getting well. Because she was so immobile, she began to develop other symptoms, including the beginnings of bed sores and water retention. In addition, though she no longer needed a ventilator, she was still suffering from the effects of acute COPD, which contributed considerably to her weakness and vulnerability. These physical ailments were further compounded by the severe anxiety she was suffering, which no amount of antianxiety drugs seemed to allay.

Given all of this, we measured success by the degree to which we were able to help her forget about her pain, and the only way to do this for an extended period was to screen a movie on a portable DVD player and watch it with her. Television proved a poor distraction—since Mom had no use for it when she was well, why would she take to it when she wasn't? But she did love movies and, in particular, she loved to watch a handful of her favorites over and over again. These included *Moonstruck*, *My Cousin Vinnie*, *Walk the Line* and, most beloved of all, *Dirty Dancing*.

My sisters and I would take turns sitting and watching these with her, and one particular afternoon my turn had come round and the movie of choice was *Dirty Dancing*. As in most things, my taste in movies was very different from my mother's, and this particular film was one I had not seen. Though it was something I would never have chosen to watch on my own, I felt happy and honored to sit beside her and see her favorite film for the first time. As the first scenes opened and the plot unfolded, I was drawn into the story, and the fact that it was about a young girl's rite of passage and independence from her mother and family struck me as poignant. The character of "Baby," the heroine, was headstrong and difficult—not unlike myself at her age. I was struck by the beauty of the actors—especially the young Patrick Swayze, who had died just a few months earlier. Here in this film he was young, athletic, and deeply handsome—so different from the cancer-ravaged man in the news so recently. I found myself mourning his loss, even as I felt the joy of his performance. This made an already emotional situation much more so—and then there was the dancing. Dance is always an expression of the inexpressible and is, therefore, a deeply moving art. The dance numbers in the film were passionate, beautiful pantomimes of the powerful emotions the characters were not able to articulate. I felt my eyes tearing up repeatedly at scenes that might seem ordinary enough, but in my emotionally raw and vulnerable state, they unfolded as achingly indicative of the pleasure and pain of life.

While I was wrestling with my emotions, trying to keep them in check, my mother was, too. At one point, midway through the film, when it seems as if Baby and the young man she loves will never get together, she turned to me and asked, in an agitated voice, "I wonder what's going to happen?" I was amazed. This is a film my mother had seen scores—perhaps hundreds—of times, and she had forgotten the ending. Her confusion and forgetfulness were clearly getting worse rather than better. The question rendered me speechless, until I murmured some words meant to comfort her, "I'm not sure, Mom. Let's watch and see." We both turned back to the film to witness a scene where Baby sits alone crying over her predicament. In response to the sight and sound of her tears, my mother, too, began wailing. At first her words were incomprehensible, but as she repeated them, over and over, I heard her say: "I miss my friend! I miss my Gene!" Then it became clear to me and to my sister Charlene, who had come into the room, that she was mourning her longtime friend and partner who had died the year before. My sister had helped her through a year of this loud, demonstrative grieving—it was, in fact, one of the catalysts that had provoked an increase in her drinking and led to her return to rehab. And now, after all of that supposed time and healing, she was back again in this place of sorrow. We allowed her to cry for a bit, to vent her feelings, and then tried and succeeded in pulling her attention back to the film. The plot unfolded, leading to the final, joyful dance, performed to the song "The Time of Your Life," wherein the lovers lay claim to each other, her parents face the reality that she is grown up, and the ending promises a lifetime of love and happiness for the pair.

At the end of the film, I was utterly exhausted, and so was Mom. She asked to be moved from her chair to her bed and promptly went to sleep. I envied her that peace—and even her forgetfulness—for I knew she would awaken unperturbed by the film and the deep well of emotion it had opened up inside her. But I would not forget. This is what beauty does to us—the beauty of the story, the music, the dance, the human body, and the human face—all of these remind us of the gift of art we give to one another to lift our minds and hearts, to open our eyes and ears, to enable us to perceive the beauty that lies in our own being, our relationships to one another, and our world. And this perception, beautiful as it may be, breaks us open and fills us with a longing we can't quite name.

"Late have I loved you, / Beauty so old and so new. / Late have I loved you." These words of St. Augustine describe the universal human search for God and the way in which beauty can lead us in the direction of the holy. In the six days of *kairos* in my mother's room, we four women were led by beauty to places we would not have gone otherwise. A few months after my mother's passing, one sacrament led to another (they are "seven times seventy," as Andre Dubus reminds us), and I wrote a poem in attempt to capture the complex, beautiful paradox of these days I spent with my mother in pursuit of beauty. It helps me to remember—and when my memory fails, as it inevitably will, I hope the poem will continue to speak what those days taught me.

Watching *Dirty Dancing* with My Mother

in the sad sleep of the nursing home,
we are both surprised by beauty alone,

by Baby's newfound ecstasy,
the passion of young Patrick Swayze

as he moves her across the bare wood,
lifts her high toward the old god of girlhood

and sets her down, more sure of her charm
each step beyond his circling arms.

Nothing can soothe her father's frown
seeing his daughter as someone now,

no more the child she cannot stay.
Patrick, too, has passed away.

None of us the beauty we used to be,
my mother, those dancers, me.[3]

Chapter 4

THE SACRAMENT OF HUMOR

*The laughter of the universe is God's delight. It is the universal
Easter laughter.*

—Jürgen Moltmann, *The Coming of God*

It may seem strange to identify humor, along with its twin
sister, laughter, as sacraments. After all, the practice of the
sacraments is a serious enterprise. We take Communion in
reverence, mindful of Christ's sacrifice; we go to Confession
humbled by our brokenness; we go to Baptisms and Confir-
mations properly awed by the welcoming of a soul made new
in Christ and renewed by the Holy Spirit; we attend weddings and ordinations well aware of the powerful nature of
the binding vows the participants will take before God and
ourselves; and we witness Last Rites in an hour of darkness as
death approaches. None of these solemn sacraments seems to
have much in common with humor.

A closer look at the nature of humor, though, reveals its deep connections with each of the "official" sacraments of the Church. In his book *The Spirituality of Imperfection*, Ernest Kurtz makes the interesting observation that "the words *human*, *humor*, and *humility* all have the same root—the Indo-European *ghôm*, best translated by the English *humus*."[1] *Humus* is a word meaning "soil" or "earth," reminding us of the creation of Adam in Genesis, of the fact that human beings are made of the stuff of earth, and of our inevitable return to that earth, for dust we are and to dust we shall return (Gn 3:19). The word "human" is derived from *humus*, returning us to the ground of our being etymologically in much the same way death does physically. The very name used to describe humankind inevitably engenders in us humility, for what fool could be proud or arrogant in the face of such a humble beginning and a humble end? The word "humor" partakes of both our humanness and our humility in that it thrives on the recognition—and even the celebration—of our flaws, our shortcomings, and our wayward tendencies as fallen human beings. Humility allows us to admit and embrace our radical imperfection, and humor lets us delight in it—both our own imperfections and those of our fellow human beings.

In *Redeeming Laughter: The Comic Dimension of Human Experience*, Peter Berger identifies humor and the comic as signals of transcendence. Humor, along with the attendant laughter it provokes, allows us to suspend the rules of the ordinary world, if only temporarily, since it takes us out of ourselves and our current situation (dire as it may be) and enables us to glimpse a consoling vision that delights. The humor may be momentary, but this "other reality" that the humor points to is not temporary at all; in fact, it highlights a world beyond our current troubles that is essentially "comic" in the sense that all will be well eventually, for all things are possible with God. This is the power of "redeeming laughter," which makes life easier to bear, in part because we know that this world is not the final conclusion.[2] In some sense, humor acknowledges a sacramental universe, a visible sign of the invisible reality of God's presence. In keeping with this generous theology, it might be argued that God gives us the gift of laughter so that we might enjoy a foretaste of heaven.

Humor serves, paradoxically, both to ground us in our humble human station and to enable us to aspire to a state of perfection we can't yet enjoy. Because of this, there is no fitter place than the sickroom for the Sacrament of Humor, where one is constantly reminded of the failings of the mortal body and where glimpses of heaven are in short supply.

Delight in the Ridiculous

The practice of this particular sacrament came easily and naturally to my sisters and me as we cared for our mother. As I've mentioned in a previous chapter, "The Sacrament of Speech," we have long been a family that loves to play with words, and play and language are essential elements of humor. As my mother's condition improved, during this extended "false dawn" wherein we believed she might actually recover from her illness, we were struck by the return of some of her old personality traits and by the humor of her observations. (Humor, it would seem, is also allied with the virtue of hope.) Along with her characteristic vanity, she also displayed signs of jealousy, irrational fear, and obsession with her beloved dogs. Strange as this may seem, the return of these tendencies cheered us because she seemed to be returning to her former self. Yet at the same time, new tendencies began to emerge in our mother—some of which ran counter to her characteristic disposition—and this brought us to the brink of delight. It meant that even in her sick bed, even in her ninth decade and after a lifetime of stubborn (mis)behavior, our mother could change—and for the better.

One of the ways we would cheer Mom up was to take pictures of her and send them, via cell phone, to our family members who weren't able to be there to visit with her. We would dress her in the clothes we had bought, comb her hair (her chic new haircut shown to advantage), pose her in her wheelchair, and ask her to smile. Each time I would hold up my cell phone to snap the picture, as if on cue, she would call out loudly, "No teeth!" And we would all break into broad smiles.

Mom's declaration was part apology and part statement of bald fact. Because she had lost so much weight in her sickness, mom's dentures no longer fit. At another time, the idea of being seen in public without her teeth would have disturbed her greatly, but this new version of our mother seemed to take this in stride as a small inconvenience in the face of all she had been through. But the really startling—and truly charming— revelation was her ability to find humor in her own absurd appearance. The trials of sickness had brought her a new conviction of her own humanity—her identity as *humus* (though she would not have articulated it this way)—a new humility, and a marvelous sense of the humor of the situation. My sisters and I could not help but laugh, no matter how many times she said this. It became a ritual, performed again and again (another quality of sacrament), as a means of acknowledging and celebrating the brokenness that connected—and connects—us all.

Mom also developed a capacity for making hilarious statements during these days. One afternoon, as Mom seemed to be napping, my sisters and I were speaking of our husbands, who were absent from the room. I've mentioned earlier that our mother could be a difficult person to get along with. Though she had been generous with our husbands over the years (we were all long married), she often gave voice to her disapproval of them and their behaviors. Some of this disapproval took the form of quiet, underground resentments that she harbored and kept to herself for decades. Others took the form of battles she waged out in the open, designed as public reprimand and for public display. With her sickness, we had noticed an abatement of unkind words about them, a willingness to talk to them whenever they called us, and a general interest in where they were and what they were doing. All of this was new. An explanation for her altered attitude soon arrived. As we were discussing our husbands, Mom opened her eyes and said to us, unprompted and with great clarity, "I used to hate them, but I love 'em all now!" Then she went back to her nap.

We were amazed. Simple, guileless—and humorous—as her formulation was, it spoke volumes. Our mother's intimations of her mortality had opened her mind and her heart and had brought her to a new understanding of her sons-in-law. Mom was able to see them, flawed creatures that they are, in a new light—that of eternity. A species of grace seemed to overtake her as she apparently viewed them in the spirit of mercy and forgiveness, the way in which God sees us rather than as human beings typically see one another. Suddenly able to look past their failings, or to see their supposed failings as akin to her own, she understood that her "hate" had been a disordered response. Ever a passionate person (as her use of these polar opposites would suggest), she could feel only love toward them now. Here was living proof of the beautiful statement attributed to French writer Leon Bloy, "There are places in the heart that do not yet exist, and into them enters suffering in order that they might have existence." And so our mother's heart had been enlarged by her pain, and a lifetime of dissatisfaction was redeemed in a single sentence, a kind of Confession, though the only people there to absolve my mother were her three astonished daughters.

HOLY FOLLY

The tradition of holy folly runs deep in Christianity and Catholicism. St. Paul reminds us in his writings that Christians are "fools for Christ," (1 Cor 4:10), a people who follow a man seen by the world as a fool—despised and rejected, demeaned and tortured, and finally crucified by his enemies. Christ's gentleness in the face of his enemies' cruelty must inevitably seem to be weakness and folly to those who cannot understand the significance of his sacrifice and its consequences.

Christ's folly is echoed by his true followers. The Church's favorite saints are perceived as fools by the world—St. Francis of Assisi removing his clothes in the marketplace, pledging his life to Lady Poverty, addressing Brother Fire before his own eyes are branded in attempt to save his sight; St. Catherine of Siena caring for plague victims with no regard for her own health or safety; St. Damien Molokai ministering to a leper colony and eventually dying of the disease. These saints are human beings we hold dear on account of their foolishness rather than despite it. They found joy in their extremity, and we find joy in their joy, for if God takes delight in fools, how can we not?

In his celebrated book *In Praise of Folly*, the great medieval scholar Erasmus reminds us of the benefits of folly as well, particularly with regard to the here and now: "It is through Folly that man can live spontaneously, unreasoningly, and it is only in this way that life can be tolerable."[3] The book adopts this ethos from the medieval carnival known as the "Feast of Fools," during which serious aspects of the institutional Church (particularly the hierarchy, with all of its powerful prelates and bishops) were subject to satire. According to Erasmus, making fun of the powerful or those seemingly better off than oneself has salutary benefits. This ethos is evident in stage comedy as well, from the Greeks to the present; the audience's laughter at the fools who walk across the stage is healing, for we recognize in the folly of others our own.

All of this reminds us that identifying folly where we find it is a deeply human enterprise (*humus*) and that it produces complex feelings in us. We feel detachment from fools as we laugh at them, but we also identify with them in some essential way, feel sympathy with them, and appreciate their inherent value. This also helps us to understand the double-edged nature of our laughter—that even as we seem to be laughing at others, we are laughing at ourselves. Through this laughter at our shared folly, we come to an appreciation of our common imperfection and our common holiness.

My mother's attitude toward other people had long been one of a barely achieved tolerance. Her lifelong habit had been to fall in love with new friends, becoming obsessed with them—sometimes to the exclusion of her own family—and then, as their novelty wore off, to gradually become disenchanted with them, fall out of love, and then try to escape them entirely. Since the latter was almost always impossible, she would then tolerate them, seeing the flaws she had so willingly overlooked during the first blush of friendship quite clearly. As my siblings and I watched these dramas unfold over the years, we saw plenty of foolishness on all sides.

It didn't surprise us, then, that our mother's relationship with her roommate at the nursing home followed this same pattern. When she first moved into the room, her roommate—a pleasant, elderly woman with her arm cradled in a sling—was already there. The woman had taken up residence in the bed by the window—prime real estate in any hospital or nursing home—so from the beginning, Mom had reason for resentment. When Mom first arrived, she was in no condition to communicate, but as the days went on and her health improved, she began to carry on brief conversations with her. She gradually found out that her roommate was recovering from a broken arm and that her prognosis for getting out of the nursing home soon was quite good (more reason for resentment). Mom was civil, almost pleasant, asking questions about the woman's family and remarking on her many doctors and visitors that seemed to come and go with great frequency. But gradually her friendly communication acquired an ironic edge—a shift that was barely perceptible, but it was part of a pattern we recognized.

One night, after carrying on a brief back-and-forth with her roommate, Mom turned to my sister Rose Ann and said, *sotto voce*, "Well, *she's* the smart one. She's got herself set up so she has access to the sink and the mirror." We looked up to see what she was referring to and, sure enough, we saw that there was a sink along with a small vanity and a mirror clearly situated on the woman's side of the room. We were struck by the humor of mom's observation. First, because of her vanity, it made sense that Mom would notice the mirror on her roommate's side of the room and the absence of one on her own. Second, the idea that the woman had schemed to get this supposed prize—a prize that was of no value to my mother, since she could not walk on her own or make use of the sink or mirror without help—was preposterous. Third, our mother had access to a sink and mirror in the bathroom located within a few feet of her bed, so she wasn't really being deprived at all. So we laughed and assured her that she wasn't missing much, and the phrase "having access to the mirror" became part of the nursing-home patter we would engage in when talking about Mom's accommodations with her.

The next morning, Mom's roommate received a very elaborate flower arrangement accompanied by an enormous Mylar balloon in the shape of a bumblebee. The flower arrangement was so large that it took up a good deal of space on the window ledge, and the outsized bee became a prominent feature of their small room. No matter where we stood, it always seemed to be in our line of sight. Mom congratulated her on the flowers as they were brought in, telling the woman that she was lucky to have family members who cared about her so much. (For the record, Mom had no flowers on her side of the room. We had not thought to bring any. As I look back on this, perhaps her comment was meant to chastise us as well as to patronize her roommate.)

For the remainder of the morning, the woman occupied herself reading and writing letters. At one point, my mother turned to her and said, "Well, aren't you lucky? You can sit there and write your letters. I can't do anything over here. I can't even think straight!" Her roommate seemed oblivious to Mom's accusatory tone, and she responded by telling my mother whom she was writing to and what she was writing about. My mother feigned interest in the woman's account.

Then she turned to me and said, in a low voice, "I wish I had a pin to *pop* that balloon!"

Once again, I had to laugh at our mother's duplicity and irritation. She had been famously impatient with her own children when we were growing up, so her attitude toward her roommate did not surprise us. This was the prickly Marion we knew and loved, and seeing her annoyed over her roommate's flowers and the way she spent her time meant, to our minds, that she was getting back to being her difficult self. For her roommate's part, she seemed to be completely fooled by our mother's seeming attentiveness. A trusting and, all around, nicer person than Mom, I'm quite sure that when she left the hospital she was none the wiser.

Watching this unfold, we were reminded of our mother's tendency toward folly. Very often, during our long, collective relationship with her, we had felt that our roles were reversed—that our mother had acted the part of the spoiled child while we served as adult onlookers, hoping she would behave better. In this situation, though, we were suddenly appreciative of our mother's childish behavior, her double-dealing, and her irony. This, after all, was who she was, and we felt gratitude for the return of her quirkiness rather than feeling judgmental or being anxious about whom she might offend.

Laughter in the Dark

That having been said, some of the humor we saw in our mother had the quality of pathos. For example, before delivering one of her ritual accounts of the suffering she had endured, she would begin with the declaration, "You don't know what I've been through!" The first few times I heard this, I would respond sympathetically in a voice that was meant to be reassuring, "I know, Mom." Her response was instantaneous: "I know *you* know, but Michal doesn't know," indicating that her granddaughter (Michal), who was present, needed to be filled in so that Mom might have her sympathy as well. (Michal, of course, knew everything that Mom had endured, but we allowed Mom the fiction that this was the first time Michal was hearing these details.)

There was also *pathos* in her regression into childhood. Each day, even as Mom was recovering, we noticed that she became more fearful. The world for her, in the past month, had gradually shrunk to the size of her nursing-home room, and venturing out into the hallways or to other parts of the nursing-home facility was traumatic. One day, Michal and I wheeled Mom over to the imaging department so her lungs could be X-rayed. As we waited, both of us standing behind her wheelchair, the technician turned out the lights in order to (somehow) facilitate the X-ray he was preparing to take. Mom immediately began screaming, begging him to turn on the lights and shouting that she was afraid of the dark. Michal was shocked by her grandmother's terror, so much so that she had a difficult time believing it was real. She laughed, assuring "Gram" that there was nothing to be afraid of, that the darkness couldn't hurt her—words very similar to those my mother once used to assure her granddaughter, twenty years earlier, and her daughter, forty years earlier. I was struck by her gentleness and by the eagerness with which my mother listened to her assurances.

In addition to this fear of the dark, my mother also developed a fear of open spaces. As we took her for walks around the nursing home in her wheelchair, she grew comfortable in the familiar corridors, but if we turned her chair toward the glass doors at the entrance of the facility or toward the large picture window in the cafeteria, Mom would become alarmed and insist that we turn around and take her back to her room. Once again, the vehemence of her objections seemed all out of proportion to what was actually taking place. She would wave her arms and cry out in an almost comically exaggerated way. This was strange and unexpected, for our mother had always loved the sun, the palm trees, and the blue skies so typical of Florida. These were the reasons she had moved there from our home in northeastern Pennsylvania thirty years ago, and to see her suddenly and unaccountably fearful of them struck us as odd, an ironic turn we never would have imagined. We tried to defuse these situations with humor, to let her know she sounded silly (much as our mother had once counseled us—and wisely) and that the outdoors were no threat to her. But we knew, even in making light of such moments, that she had crossed an invisible line—that this woman who had long loved the out-of-doors, the beach, the sun, the color of the sky, had become a virtual shut-in, clinging to the comforts and the security of the nursing home and rejecting the life that lay beyond its doors.

SURPRISED BY JOY

There are many uses and functions of humor. It comes quite naturally to us in moments of joy, but it comes to us in moments of uncertainty as well. The greatest writers and poets— Dante, Chaucer, Shakespeare—understood that comedy and tragedy cannot be separated, for both are part of the seamless fabric of human life. Their poems and plays are full of moments of humor, even in the midst of catastrophe. Young Hamlet cracks jokes, even as he mourns the death of his father and the hasty marriage of his beloved mother to an uncle he despises. The humor offers some relief, if only momentarily, to his suffering. The dark humor of fiction writer Flannery O'Connor reminds us that even in moments of extremity, human beings perceive humor and may even chastise themselves for doing so. And yet there is a kind of strength in seeing the irony in one's own situation. It allows us an alternate perspective from which to view our pain.

This was often the case with us during the course of the final forty-eight days of my mother's life. At some junctures, our humor was akin to whistling in the dark as one passes by the graveyard—an attempt at bravado in the face of our own fears. Most of the time, however, our humor was an expression of joy—an involuntary response to an outbreak of the unexpected, an incongruity, or a reversal.

Perhaps my favorite instance of the latter was the sight of our eighty-two-year-old mother flirting with the young, male orderly who took care of her some evenings. Our Mom had always been pretty and had long enjoyed receiving the attention of men. Though she was confused by her medications and racked by her pain, it was a source of sweetness to see her ability to forget about these afflictions in the presence of this young man and to seek his attention. We saw glimpses of her former (if flawed) self, a reason for celebration. From the first time she met the orderly, she made her preferences for his attention clear, and she would tell him how handsome he was when he would come into her room. For his part, he received these attentions with patience and kindness (a fact I remain grateful for).

During one such evening, he had occasion to lift Mom out of her wheelchair and place her in her bed, a procedure he carried out with great care and gentleness. As he was lifting her up, my mother reached up, placing her arms around his neck, and kissed him, after which she announced, "I love you!" The orderly smiled and thanked her, settled her comfortably into her bed, and then left the room. My sisters and I were much moved by our mother's honesty and willingness to wear her heart on her proverbial sleeve. The scene was funny, by any measure—the incongruity of an old woman doting over a man young enough to be her grandson—but it was also sweet, endearing, and deeply human. Here was our mother, making a fool of herself over the beauty of this young man (she had ever been a fool for beauty), and we were lucky enough to witness it and to be surprised by joy—both hers and our own.

In his book *The Coming of God*, theologian Jürgen Moltmann writes, "The laughter of the universe is God's delight. It is the universal Easter laughter."[4] Moltmann reminds us that laughter is a promise and a sign of resurrection. Even in our greatest trials and darkest sorrows, laughter reminds us that good will triumph over evil, light over darkness, and life over death. We apprehend this spiritual fact with our minds and express it with our bodies in the (absurd) physical experience of laughing—our very flesh enacting and embodying the inward Easter we feel. Laughter is infectious and communal—we rarely engage in it alone—and we laughed often in our mother's sickroom. It served as a shared sacrament—along with its twin sister, humor—as an outward expression of our implicit faith. Thinking back on those days and weeks and hours with her, I now understand that when we were laughing, we were practicing resurrection.

Chapter 5

The Sacraments of the Cell Phone and the Wheelchair

I told her that tomorrow I would tell my father I loved him. Before dawn he died, and for years I regretted not saying the words. But I did not understand love then, and the sacraments that make it tactile. I had not lived enough and lost enough to enable me to know the holiness of . . . moving on wheels or wings or by foot from one place to another; of holding a telephone and speaking into it and listening to a voice.

—Andre Dubus, "Sacraments"[1]

The concept of the cell phone as sacramental object is, perhaps, not a surprising idea. For many modern Americans, their cell phones (and, in particular, their smartphones) are their most prized and revered possessions. We pay enormous amounts of money for the phones themselves, as well as the calling plans, and we spend enormous amounts of time consulting them for information, communicating with them via calls and texts, engaging in social media with them, and simply gazing at the (tiny) screens in rapt wonderment. Our cell phones are, in complex ways, tied up with our identity. Our precious private information is stored in them: Social Security numbers, bank account numbers, names and numbers of our family members and acquaintances, and access to our e-mail and Facebook accounts. It's no wonder, then, that we guard them so closely, check for them frequently, and consult them throughout the day. Part oracle and part talisman, our cell phones reveal time, place, and circumstance to us—tell us where to go, what to do, how to think, whom to call, and why the sky is blue (if we take the time to Google it). They are a lifeline to the world, removing us from isolation and connecting us to much of what we value and most of those we love. Everywhere we might go, we take our beloveds with us, stored in this miraculous machine no bigger than a human hand. Is it any wonder we treat it with a kind of reverence?

The cell phone is a means of delivering us from limitation, and it makes sense that it is most valuable to us when we are most limited. Thus, in the hospital room and the nursing home, the bed-bound person with a cell phone in her hand savors the liberty and the connection it provides—with an intensity a freely roving soul can only imagine.

COMMUNICATION, COMMUNION, AND COMMUNITY

One of the daily rituals our mother most enjoyed in the nursing home was the daily round of calls we would make to those members of our family who could not be present to her physically. We would wait for a time when she was reasonably alert and free of anxiety—usually early in the day—and ask her whom she would like to talk to. If she didn't immediately name someone, we would scroll through the names of people in her contacts, reading them off, until we arrived at a person she was eager to speak to. Once she identified him or her, we would punch in the phone number, get the person on the line, tell the person that Mom was calling, and then place the phone at her ear. Most of the calls lasted only a few minutes since she would tire quickly. The call would consist mostly of an update on her symptoms and condition, a report of her breakfast or lunch, and words of encouragement that she would gladly receive from the person she had called. Then she would hand the phone back to us, and we would conclude the call, telling the person (loudly) that Mom was doing much better and she would probably call back tomorrow. She would then take a brief rest, and we would repeat the ritual as many times as she wanted us to.

These calls served, for our family members and her friends, as virtual visits—and for my mother as well. It helped to remind her of the people who cared about her well-being. The cell phone made them present to her in perhaps the most distinctive way we can be present to our fellow human beings—through the agency of the human voice. Our voices are distinctive, as are the rhythms of our speech. They are what mark us, perhaps more than anything else, as who we are—as a sort of aural fingerprint that identifies us beyond question. Thus, there is an intimacy to a phone call that a card, a vase of flowers, or an e-mail can never provide. We share an essential aspect of ourselves.

This phone-call ritual also provided the access to community that sacramental experience requires. It takes at least two people to carry on a phone conversation. (I am reminded of the scripture passage here: "Wherever two or three are gathered together in my name, there I am in the midst of them" [Mt 18:20].) Given my mother's limitations, we all participated in each phone call, from start to finish, thus transforming the event into a full-scale (and nearly physical) visit. Even after the phone call was finished, we would discuss what was said, bringing that person into the continually unfolding conversation that we carried on in my mother's room. As the number of people we spoke to increased, the gathering soon went far beyond the requisite "two or three" to constitute a small but mighty church.

One of the people my mother most enjoyed talking to was her sister (my aunt) Dorothy. A few years younger than my mother, Dorothy was one of my mother's five sisters. Mom had had a complicated relationship with her siblings throughout her life, and Dorothy had proven to be among the most loyal and forgiving of her sisters. She understood Mom's idiosyncrasies (she has a few herself) and found humor and *pathos* in them rather than reason to disdain or judge her. Characteristically, Aunt Dorothy was generous with her time during my mother's illness. She welcomed our frequent phone calls and would engage in conversation with Mom as long and as often as she liked.

I remember one particular call we made to Aunt Dorothy after Mom had had a difficult night. Haunted by the certainty of her own mortality, she had developed increased levels of anxiety and felt especially lonely and frightened during the nighttime hours. Aunt Dorothy, sensing and understanding her fears, assured my mother that she was never alone—that those people they most loved and who had passed away into the next world were right alongside her in her suffering. She told her that Mom's husband (my father) Charlie was there in her room with her, along with Aunt Dorothy's husband (my Uncle Bob), their mother and their father (Luigi and Anna Salvi), and their brother Sam. The idea of these loving, supernatural presences being available to her, night and day, was very comforting to my mother. Aunt Dorothy communicated this vision of watchful attentiveness with such cheerful certainty and conviction that my mother could not help but be cheered by it herself. Though we did not articulate it at the time, my sisters and I understood this to be our aunt's homely expression of the Catholic concept of the Communion of Saints. Though their beloved husbands, parents, and siblings were no longer present bodily, their seeming absence did not mean they were beyond communication. Aunt Dorothy encouraged my mother to talk to them (a form of prayer), asking for their assistance and their strength to get her through this difficult passage in her life.

The Sacrament of the Cell Phone was one species of the larger Sacrament of Communication that became so essential to my mother during this period of (seeming) recovery. The words "communication," "communion," and "community" all share the same Latin root, *communis*, meaning "held in common." All three imply the concept of oneness or unity, emphasizing our radical similitude—the fact that we are all walking the same road of life, sharing the same beginning, the same experiences of joy and desolation, and finally the same end. Since no one knows for certain what death is, that end is mysterious and inevitably frightening, and though we have to endure it alone, there is no reason we can't be accompanied by those who love us as far as is humanly possible. The company we keep as we make the journey enables us to escape the prison of selfhood and selfishness. Thus, the cell phone eased our mother's sense of loneliness and isolation. It opened up her world, if only in five-to-seven-minute increments, so that it became larger than the limits of her body and the nursing-home room she was confined to, enabling a kind of mental and spiritual travel beyond the four walls that had become both her sanctuary and her prison.

THE MERCY OF MOVEMENT

Related to this idea of the Sacrament of Communication as a means of transcendence is the concept of the Sacrament of Transportation. Just as my mother needed contact with the outside world to move beyond the walls of herself and her room, she needed physical movement to do so as well. Movement typically signifies progress, improvement, and the sense of a trajectory taking the patient to a better, more healthful state. Seen through the metaphor of pilgrimage, movement along the road in the direction of one's destination is a sign of faith, hope, and endurance even in the face of considerable obstacles. Stasis, on the other hand, signifies a kind of death, medically speaking—a state wherein there is no change, no development, and no promise of future life (at least as we know it). The still pilgrim has paused in her journey toward God, risking distraction and the possibility of losing momentum that she may never regain.

The primary obstacle to movement for my mother was the fact that she had a broken hip and could not walk. Though the hip had been surgically repaired, it still gave her a great deal of pain. Her attempts at physical therapy had all ended in the same way—with her failure to walk even with a walker, with her weeping and crying out in agony, and with her physical therapist giving up on her and leaving her in peace.

(Watching this repeated ritual—which seemed decidedly unsacramental in nature because of the way it took from her instead of nourished her and tried her instead of blessed her— was painful to us since it demonstrated quite clearly that our mother lacked the will to get stronger, as well as the physical ability.) In addition, Mom had two bad knees that would also need surgery before she could walk without pain—surgery she was not nearly strong enough to survive. Thus, this necessary movement seemed utterly impossible for her but, happily, it was not—for my mother had a wheelchair.

The wheelchair is often thought of as a sign of limitation, disability, and dependence, but we saw it very differently. After the experience of being confined to her room and to her hospital bed and of being connected to a respirator, an IV, and a heart monitor, the introduction of the wheelchair into Mom's life signified freedom, gave her the ability to move about, and stood as a symbol of her independence from the machines she once needed to keep her alive. More ancient and less sophisticated in its technology than the cell phone, the wheelchair offered us similar opportunities for community, ritual, and daily joy, reminding us that even the most homely and humble objects can serve a sacramental purpose.

Just as we set aside designated time for ritual calling, we also set aside time for daily wheelchair walks with my mother through the corridors of the nursing home. Before we would leave the room, we would engage in a ritual of preparation. Mom wanted to be sure that she was well dressed, that her hair was combed, and that she had some makeup on before we went out into the world. Then we would set out, often with no particular destination in mind. In the language of pilgrimage, the journey was its own end.

Moving together down the hallways, we would remark on the sights we would pass—the people we would see, the rooms we would glance into briefly as we wheeled by, the weather outside the windows. Our brief forays gave her some mental stimulation, brought us some novelty, and gave us something to talk about. Sometimes Mom felt well enough to stop off at the game room, where patients and their families were gathered around the television or seated at tables playing games. On one particular occasion, my niece and I played a game of dominoes with Mom (insofar as she could participate), giving her a chance to forget about something other than her pain for a while. Inevitably, though, Mom would grow restless and we would move on.

One thing I would repeatedly find on these walks is that movement would feed in her the desire for more movement. It sometimes got to the point where she couldn't abide standing still. This cheered me, in some sense, since it reminded me of my mother as she used to be. Mom had always been a dynamo, a small person who moved quickly and ably through the house, picking up after her five children, dusting, sweeping, sipping coffee, and chatting on the phone—often all at the same time. Even at meals, Mom wouldn't stay stationary. She often ate at the kitchen counter while we were seated at the table, most likely because it enabled her to keep moving even while she was eating. As Mom used to say, "I'm not a sitter"—words that struck me as ironic more than once as I wheeled her through the halls in her chair. She may have been forced to sit, but she wouldn't be forced to sit still.

The wheelchair served as a means of pleasant diversion, but it also served the practical function of conveyance when Mom needed to be taken for medical tests. At these times, our journey was not a joy ride but, rather, a version of the Stations of the Cross. We would move from X-ray to imaging to physical therapy—destinations my mother dreaded since they entailed uncomfortable and sometimes agonizing procedures. Nonetheless, she endured them, and more readily when her family took her to these places she needed to go. We tried to calm her fears, to prevail on the technician to be gentle and patient, and to make the invasive medical procedures a little more humane. I'm quite sure our mother was less terrified than she would have been had an anonymous nurse or orderly accompanied her on these journeys, and we were grateful to be helpful to her in some way.

It was at these times that my mother (and we) would feel the limitations of the marvelous chair that had given her some freedom. Though she tried to resist being taken to these places, she had no power over her own locomotion. More than once I thought of the words Jesus said to Peter when he appeared to him after the Resurrection: "Very truly I tell you, when you were younger you dressed yourself and went where you wanted; but when you are old you will stretch out your hands, and someone else will dress you and lead you where you do not want to go" (Jn 21:18). As a woman formerly in possession of a tremendous will and strong opinions, as well as the physical ability to act on her choices, our mother felt painfully her powerlessness and her predicament. Even though we were transporting her to all of these places in her best interest—the hospital, the nursing home, the physical therapist—I know my mother must have felt betrayed by us. Yet the destination we are all headed toward, in the end, is a place none of us truly wants to go to—and in our mother's resistance, we foresaw our own future and the limitations we, too, will someday endure.

LESSONS FROM THE MASTERS

Writer Andre Dubus, who was confined to a wheelchair for the last thirteen years of his life, has written beautifully about the limitations of living in a wheelchair. In his essay "Bodily Mysteries," he describes the struggle of getting up in the morning, preparing himself for Mass, driving his car to church, negotiating the doors to enter, praying for patience and strength, and finally bearing witness to the Eucharist. He writes, "Peace of mind came to me and, yes, happiness, too, for I was no longer a broken body alone in my chair. I was me, all of me, in wholeness of spirit."[2] The oneness Dubus felt with his fellow parishioners, as they processed to the altar and received the Body of Christ, relieved him from his state of isolation. He recognized that all of them were flawed and broken, some more visibly than others, and all came to receive the Eucharist in search of the wholeness they had lost. His wheelchair, as well as his own "broken body," thus became an outward sign of the brokenness we all share.

This sacramental moment is reminiscent of the heavenly procession depicted in a story written by another fine Catholic writer, Flannery O'Connor. In "Revelation," the main character in the story, Ruby Turpin, is recovering from a harrowing experience wherein she has been forced to see her flaws. Previously, Mrs. Turpin had believed herself to be one of God's chosen, saved and destined for heaven. The new vision of herself she has received suggests that, despite all of her efforts, she is no more beloved by God than the people she regards as far beneath her own state of sanctity and virtue. This point comes home to her fully—and painfully—as she experiences a kind of waking vision of the procession of the saints: at the head of the line are the halt and the lame, the most limited and broken among us, while she and her husband are stuck firmly in the back at the very end of the line.

Both of these stories—Dubus's and O'Connor's—came to me often while I pushed my mother in her wheelchair through the corridors of the hospital. Her limitation made me aware of the strength of body I now enjoyed but also of the inevitable loss of that strength. My brokenness was embedded in me, as it is in all of us. My strong mother, who had once pushed me in a baby carriage, a stroller, and a grocery cart, was no longer capable of pushing me, so it was my turn to push her—just as I, too, will one day need the strong arms of one of my children to push me along. This Sacrament of the Wheelchair served as a kind of communion for us. I don't know if she was aware enough to feel the sense of unity and wholeness Dubus describes, but I hope and pray she was. We moved up and down those hallways as one, two parts of a single whole. "Peace of mind came to me and, yes, happiness, too." I believe she shared in that peace and happiness as well, if only for a few moments.

The moment in O'Connor's story struck me in an almost humorous way, mostly because of the physical posture one assumes when pushing a wheelchair: the disabled person rides in the front while the able-bodied person walks in the back behind her. In "Revelation," Ruby Turpin witnesses a literal illustration of the biblical maxim, "For the last shall be first and the first will be last" (Mt 20:16). I felt as if I, too, were receiving that same lesson.

For much of my adult life, I had been troubled by my mother's flaws and failures to live what I believed to be an acceptable life. She smoked too much, she drank too much, she cursed too much, and she liked the company of men too much. Meanwhile, I had been living what I thought to be a virtuous life, trying to be a faithful wife and attentive mother, a dedicated teacher, and a truthful writer. But in the end, as I watched my mother grow weaker, put away her habits and personality traits, and become fully human, I knew that she was beloved of her Creator as much as, or more than, the most seemingly observant of believers. As I pushed her through the halls of the nursing home, I knew it was fitting that she be first and I be last. And this, too, brought me peace and made me happy.

Chapter 6

THE SACRAMENT OF WITNESS

*Then he came to the disciples and found them sleeping; and he
said to Peter,
"Could you not stay awake with me one hour?"*
—Matthew 26:40

The last conversation I had with my mother while she was still
conscious, on the morning of January 18, was full of promise.
Though her condition had not markedly improved, during
the six days I was with her it had not deteriorated, and I took
this to be a good sign. I explained to my mother that I had to
go back to New York to begin a new semester of teaching, but
I assured her I would be back for her birthday on February
15—exactly four weeks away. Her response to this news was
strangely evasive. Instead of acknowledging my departure, she
looked off to the other side of the room, pretending not to
hear me. When she did turn her attention to me, she spoke of

her daily round, how she felt, and whom she was planning to call that day, but she remained silent about my leaving.

My farewell was not only one-sided, but it was also more permanent than I had imagined it to be. I had no way of knowing this was the last time I would hear her voice or that she would die on February 1, well before the birthday celebration I foolishly anticipated. Though I would be fortunate to spend her last hours with her in the hospice ward—a blessing for which I will always be grateful—my mother would be unconscious by the time I arrived. It still pains me to think that my mother never said goodbye to me.

However, as I think back on the day we parted, farewells and birthdays were two rituals that my mother disliked. There is a part of me that knows she knew I was going and that we might not meet again—this would explain her silence, her refusal to acknowledge that this might be true, and it allows me to see her denial as a manifestation of her reluctance to let me go. There is also a part of me that knows she was tired of birthdays. Two years earlier, when we tried to throw her an elaborate family party to celebrate her eightieth birthday, Mom warned us that she would not come. We planned it anyway, thinking that at the last minute she would relent. She didn't. We ended up having to go through with the party without her. This was her way of letting us know she was opting out of birthdays. Tired of getting older with every passing year, she must have been attracted by the idea of skipping out before another one came around, a small victory against the inexorable onslaught of time she had mightily resisted for much of her life.

While I returned to my ordinary life—and my sister Rose Ann returned to her job and family in north Florida—my sister Charlene remained to care for my mother. Suddenly, the labor that three of us had shouldered shifted to one person: the daily and nightly visitation, the consultation with doctors, the endless correspondence with insurance companies, and the daily challenges presented by my mother's illness. The rituals we had developed to allay Mom's fears became more difficult to carry out alone, and the demands of my sister's own busy family life increased the burden on her. When I spoke with her on the phone, I could hear the exhaustion in her voice and her concern over Mom's increasingly troubling symptoms, especially her acute anxiety that no medication remedied. As she became more and more mired in her sickness, our mother's body began to deteriorate rapidly, and even the most vigilant daughter could not have foreseen and fought off the inexorable progress of mortality.

On January 31, a snowy Sunday morning in New York, my sister called to tell me our mother was back in the hospital. She had been rushed to the emergency room the day before when her vital signs began failing; after her admittance to the hospital, my sister learned that our mother was suffering from a systemic infection. My other sister had joined her—they had been watching her for twenty-four hours—and it was now becoming clear that she was not going to recover. Though we did not realize it at the time, this was the beginning of yet another sacramental observance, that of bearing witness, conducting the ritual watch over a dying person.

PRESENCE

Bearing witness is a watch, but it is also more than that. The word "watch" implies passivity, a waiting for something to happen. The experience my sisters and I shared with my mother in her last days and hours, however, was anything but passive. Indeed, we were full participants in the drama that unfolded, accompanying our mother toward the next stage of her journey, preparing the way, getting her ready, and responding to her needs. As with any sacrament, bearing witness is an act one must be fully awake for (as Christ reminds his disciples). Even the experience of watching takes on a participatory quality as one observes the events unfolding and the myriad signs and symbols, each detail requiring attention, articulation, and interpretation.

Our telephone conversations over the next night and day reflected this heightened awareness as my sisters relayed to me the many details of Mom's last hours. Among these is a story my sister told of one of the (supposed) delusions my mother suffered as she lapsed in and out of consciousness. She imagined herself to be cooking a pot of spaghetti—something our mother did for us thousands of times—but she worried it would get too soft (the most egregious of culinary errors in an Italian household). Charlene assured her that the consistency was perfect. After the ritual stirring and tasting, Mom said she was hungry but that the door of her stomach needed to be opened. My sister dutifully did this for her, miming the unlocking of the door, the grasp of the knob, the movement of the hinge. "Is that better?" she asked. "Much better!" Mom answered. She asked for pasta with tomato sauce, no meatballs, but lots of cheese. My sister complied, serving my mother her imaginary meal, and my mother gratefully chewed her fugitive food. The poignancy of this scene—one I never witnessed but have imagined many times since my sister described it to me—still touches me deeply. My sister's love and attention, her willingness to provide our mother with spiritual sustenance, renders the meal sacramental—yet another incarnation of Eucharist. The sharing of this meal was part and parcel of all the meals they shared in the course of their lives, those served at the altar of the church and those enjoyed at the altar of the family table—both arenas and both species of meals sacred to our lives.

I find it moving that, shortly after this moment, my mother's parish priest came to her room to hear her confession and give her Holy Communion. Receiving these official sacraments cheered my mother enormously. Having been denied Communion for much of her life on account of her divorce at the age of seventeen and her civil marriage to our father, she now could enjoy complete union with the Church. Her long lifetime of faithfulness (in her fashion) had, at last, issued in her being embraced once more by the institution that she loved. (I believe she always knew herself to be loved by God—despite the Church's exclusion of her from Communion. She knew this to be a decision made by men and not by Christ.) As he was leaving, the priest told my sister, "Your mother will go straight to heaven." I don't know if our mother overheard this, but if she did, I'm quite sure of what her thoughts must have been: "Of course I will!" Our mother was that confident in her basic goodness and in the certainty of God's mercy.

The sacraments dispensed to my mother during those days and hours were numberless. They took many forms, and they were often dispensed by my sisters. In pondering all of this, from a distance, in the days after my sister shared these stories, I wrote a poem portraying that reality (another enactment of the Sacrament of Speech and engagement in the Sacrament of Distance).

REAL PRESENCE

for Charlene

*The priest came this morning
and gave me Holy Communion,*
she said, as if we ought to be
impressed that Christ

was at her bedside,
in her hand,
            on her tongue
an hour before and gone.

He keeps coming and going,
            she said, *from room to room,*
the Indian River Nursing Home
become Jesus' favorite haunt

according to our mother,
a lapsed Catholic
            school-girl forever
            seeing God.

Then he walked in again,
wearing a skirt, a black jacket,
and sling-back high-heel shoes,
looking remarkably like my sister.

He sat with her for hours,
heard her litany of fears,
fed her dinner,
adjusted her Depends.

They watched *Moonstruck*,
then danced a brief
wheelchair dance,
a final *Tarantella* for the road.

I'll always love you,
Johnny Cammareri,
Mom confessed and kissed
Christ on the lips.

He cried with her when she cried
for her dead friends.
He stroked her ancient face,
called her beautiful, and meant it.

He promised not to leave her.
He never did.[1]

PILGRIMAGE

On the morning of February 1, my sisters called with the news that our mother had been moved to hospice care. Despite the intensive medical care she had received in the hospital, her condition continued to deteriorate. The doctors acknowledged they could do no more for her. She might survive a few days or a matter of hours—it wasn't clear. But one thing that was clear was my need to get there as quickly as I could.

That afternoon at 1:25, I boarded a flight from Westchester County Airport to West Palm Beach, landed at 4:30, and then was driven along the rain-soaked roads by my sister's husband, Rick, to the hospice center in Vero Beach. During the drive, we called my sisters to see if we might stop along the way for a quick bite. (In my hurry to catch my flight, I had forgotten entirely to eat.) "No. Come now," my sister Charlene said. "And hurry. She's waiting for you." I had traveled the thousand-mile distance to be by my mother's side several times in the past forty-eight days, but this was the first time I sensed the urgency and the necessity of my arrival. My sister had pronounced those words, "She's waiting for you," calmly, matter-of-factly, and with great certainty. This time there was no doubt about the outcome of the visit: I was making a pilgrimage, engaging in a quest, the goal of which was to be present to my mother as she passed out of this world. It felt like a calling, one I was honored to receive and grateful to have heard and heeded.

Traveling toward my destination with such deliberate purpose, I reflected on the common pilgrimage my mother, my sisters, and I had all been engaged in for the past five decades. From the moment each of us was conceived and then born, all of our collective experiences, across time and space, had led us, amazingly and miraculously, to this single moment. She had seen us come into the world, had guided us through our lives, and now it was our turn to help her take leave of it. It was as if the broad river of time was narrowing down to a thin stream, and all of us were being borne along to a single point of departure. We were conscious, in our way, of wanting to ease her passage and of assuring her that we were present and that all would be well, both with us and with her.

As I traveled down the interstate and those dark back roads, I was conscious of the strange fact that I was relieved, rather than fearful, about bearing witness to her passing. I felt as if we were preparing for a birth as well as a death, a cessation of one kind of life and the beginning of another. Though I knew we would be beset by unspeakable sorrow when she died, I also knew that she would be released from unbearable suffering. My mother had been unwell and un-happy for so many years, and so I felt quite certain that the life she was tending toward would be better than the one she had been living. The prayers that I said silently to myself were that she would not suffer pain in making her passage and that she would not be afraid. I also prayed that she would still be alive when I arrived, for I had much to say to her.

PRACTICE

We arrived at the hospice center at 7:15, and as my brother-in-law and I walked into my mother's room, I was amazed to find my two sisters sitting calmly on the side of my mother's bed, smiling and talking to her. She was heavily sedated, deep in an opium sleep, but my sisters talked to her as if she could hear everything they said. "Guess what, Mom? Angela's here!" my sister Charlene announced happily. Then she turned to me, still smiling, and said, "We've been waiting for you." I was overwhelmed with gratitude, both at these welcoming words and at the fact that Mom was still with us.

I immediately sat down on the bed, took her left hand in mine, and told her how happy I was to see her. Though she could not acknowledge me, I had the strong, strange sensation that she knew I was there, knew exactly what was go-ing on, and was prepared for whatever would happen in that room. I also had the sensation that we had all been preparing for these final hours together for a very long time—that our lives from the very beginning had been a long rehearsal for this parting: going to church together as children, suffering disappointment and tragedy together, experiencing a lifetime of joy together, and preparing and sharing innumerable meals together. Each of these moments constituted practice for this most significant event.

There is no rule book for a death watch. No one tells us the etiquette of how to accompany the dying. Every family must create its own practice, depending on their dispositions, their relationships, and the circumstances of the person's passing. The particulars of our practice were few but significant. It had all the signs of sacramental observance. For instance, my sister had brought a bottle of wine to Mom's room, along with four long-stemmed glasses from her kitchen at home. Each was painted artfully with a lovely flower—a blue hydrangea, a peach-colored tulip, a pink plum blossom, and a red rose. (Here was the Sacrament of Beauty in the sickroom, yet again, and though Mom could not appreciate its presence in her current state, it allayed some of our pain.)

Having discharged his duty in bringing me from the airport, Rick poured himself a sip of wine, lifted his glass in my mother's direction, and offered a toast along with a deeply touching farewell. His gesture was both ceremonial and personal, the repetition of a ritual they had engaged in many times in the course of the forty years they had known each other. It occurred to me that my mother's favorite toast had long been "*Salute!*"—the Italian wish for "good health"—a phrase that struck me as painful in our present circumstances. (Notably, my brother-in-law omitted this from his toast.) Then he drank the wine, set down his glass, and left the four of us together.

At last, I had the chance to really look at my mother. Strange to say, encountering her in this state was less of a shock than it had been when I arrived to find her in intensive care before her operation and when I arrived to find her in the nursing home afterward. No longer hooked up to invasive machinery, no longer tormented by the anxiety and pain associated with her illness, she seemed to be at peace. Her skin was so white that it seemed translucent, as if light could come through it. It made her seem fragile, precious, and youthful. Images of ivory and porcelain come to mind as I recall her other-worldly still-ness, the silky perfection of her unlined forehead. She slept so deeply—it reminded me of the untroubled sleep of infants. She breathed heavily, as if air was all she loved and needed now. The words "breath of life" occurred to me then, taking on more meaning than they'd ever had before.

I was also amazed at how warm her hand was in mine. It was soft and supple as a child's, despite her eighty-two years. Twined around her right hand, which lay quietly at her side, was a rosary—a set of "travel" beads I had lent to my sister Rose Ann once when she was boarding a flight from the air-port in New York. I had passed them on to her, a sacramental to calm her fears and to keep her safe on her journey, and now Rose had given them to our mother as she was setting out on her own journey. Passed from sister to sister and from daugh-ter to mother, the beads' history gave them added significance.

When my sisters left the room, taking a short break from the labor of keeping watch, I found myself alone with my mother for what would be the last time. This was my oppor-tunity to say the things to her I had left unsaid for so long. I told her how much I loved her and that I wished I had been a better daughter. For many years, I had been an in-frequent visitor—since traveling to Florida is an expensive and time-consuming trip for a young couple with three small children—but I knew these to be excuses. We were such dif-ferent people who seemed to share so little in common, that neglecting her was easier than faithfulness. I had tried to make amends in subsequent years, but the damage had been done;

the relationship remained strained and distant and difficult. I realize now, as I recall my urgent need to unburden myself of this accumulated guilt I had been carrying for so long, that my last conversation with my mother was deeply sacramental, a form of confession. These were "sins" of which only she could absolve me, and though she was unable to acknowledge my profound apologies, I felt quite certain she could hear me and that she forgave me.

I also told her I had been writing poems about her for years and that I read them regularly at poetry readings, where I spoke of her honestly and with great affection. (Mom had never been a conventional mother, and in my poems I try to honor the woman she was rather than the one I might have wished her to be.) As a result of this, many of my friends and acquaintances had come to love and to admire her. Just as I learned to value her quirks and imperfections as indispensable, part of the imprint of her personality, so did they. As I confessed all of this to her, I realized that I had, unwittingly, devised a form of penance for my sins of omission—that my poetry had functioned as sacrament in more ways than I knew.

When my sisters returned to the room, the conversation became communal once again. I was reminded of the patter we had practiced when Mom was first hospitalized, shortly after she had broken her hip. We spoke cheerfully of everyday matters—the weather, the whereabouts of our children, the kindness of the hospice staff—addressing ourselves to our mother as well as one another, as if she were a full (if silent) participant in the conversation. For the next three hours we sat our watch, adjusted her pillow, stroked her face, and held her hand, knowing that we were waiting until her moment of readiness arrived.

At 10:15 p.m., my cell phone rang. My youngest son, Will, was calling from home to ask how my journey had been and to see how his grandmother was. After a few minutes, I asked him if he'd like to speak to her, and when he said yes, I put the phone to her ear. I heard him tell her that he missed her, that he hoped she would be better soon, and that he loved her. I took the phone back then and told him that I would call him later. As he was speaking to her, I noticed Mom's breathing had slowed.

We gathered around the bed, listening intently, as her breaths grew shallower and shallower—and then she didn't breathe anymore. It was not so much a struggle as it was a surrender—a quiet giving over of the battle she had fought for the past forty-eight days. I felt for her pulse, since I still was holding her left hand, and found that her heart was still beating. It was then that we told her that it was okay for her to go—that we loved her and would see her again. She passed so peacefully we could not be sure of the exact moment she died. Gradually, we noticed her mouth drop open, and how still and empty her face was, and we knew that the spirit of life had left her.

Our watch had come to an end. We had accompanied her on her journey as far as we could. Now it was time to grieve.

THE ANTI-SACRAMENT OF GRIEF

And grieve we did.

When my mother's spirit left the room, my sisters and I wept like children. All the pent-up fear and pity and sorrow we had carried within us came out—tears not only for the past forty-eight days but also for the many years of our lives together. And yet we grieved differently. My sister Rose lamented as I had never heard her before, heaving wordless, breathless sobs. My sister Charlene wept and spoke through tears, stroking my mother's face and telling her, poignantly, "You were my best friend." I wept quietly, almost inwardly, as if the brute fact of what had transpired was not yet real to me. I felt as if this loss were familiar rather than fresh—as if I had lost my mother before and was now losing her yet again.

The wildness of grief is the opposite of sacrament. Grief threatens to dismantle us along with the reality we have constructed and by which we live. Sacrament builds and affirms that reality. Perhaps this is why, in the midst of unspeakable sorrow, there is healing in turning to rituals. After our initial outburst of sorrow, after we called in the hospice nurses to confirm our mother's death, and after they hugged us and held us and offered their heartfelt condolences, my sisters and I calmed ourselves and resumed our watch around our mother. We bore witness to each minute change in her body. Her face, which had been soft and supple, gradually grew bone-hard and immobile. Her hands grew stiff and gradually lost their warmth. We removed her gold chain from around her neck and her Rosary from her hand. We covered her up and tucked the blanket gently beneath her shoulders. We smoothed her black hair, still cut in the smart bob Rose had given her a few short weeks ago, and we each kissed her cheek, now cold as soapstone.

"She looks like a saint," my sister Rose said as we stood around her bed and looked our last time upon the face we had all loved so much. And Rose was right—even in death, she shone. As it turned out, this was the last glimpse we were to have of our mother.

Then we signed the papers, consigned her body to the morgue, and left the room. Somehow it pained me, just before the door closed, that the hospice nurse reached for the switch to shut out the light, leaving our mother in the dark.

And then, because there was nothing more we could do, we went home.

Chapter 7

THE SACRAMENT OF HONOR

Honor thy father and thy mother:
that thy days may be long upon the land which the Lord *thy God*
giveth thee.
—Exodus 20:12

After my mother's death, the biblical injunction to "honor thy father and thy mother" suddenly struck me as powerful, poignant, and profound. Death radically changes one's relationship to the departed. Once the beloved has passed on, the care of her body, her memory, and her legacy are placed entirely in the hands of the living. In a very practical way, the dead depend on us. When the dearly departed is your mother—the person who carried you for nine months, pushed you into the world, and cared for you at the most vulnerable stages of your existence—an already hefty weight of awe and obligation considerably increases.

I became alarmingly aware of the need to do everything right. The rituals of the wake, the funeral, and the burial lay ahead, along with those less formal rites of notifying family and friends, writing Mom's obituary, preparing and delivering her eulogy, planning a funeral supper, and taking care of her belongings. In the days, weeks, and months ahead, we would need to discover how to accomplish these things in a way that would bring honor to our mother. I realize in retrospect that we knew them to be sacraments—rather than chores to be checked off a list—very much in keeping with those we had been practicing for the previous forty-eight days. Thus began a new chapter in our sacramental making, along with a new phase of the journey that we were taking with her. We believed our long pilgrimage together had ended at her deathbed the night before, but in the Florida morning light of February 2, we woke to the knowledge that we still had a ways to go.

WAKING OUR MOTHER

We did not wake our mother when she died.

The night before, after her soul parted from her body in her hospice room, my sisters and I had left her body behind for the staff—experts at handling the dead—to take care of. "Where will she go?" I asked the kind nurse, who had hugged me and my sisters long and hard after she verified the absence of our mother's heartbeat.

"To the morgue," she replied—reluctantly, I thought. "In the basement."

We knew that our mother, who had moved to Florida to escape the freezing winters of northeastern Pennsylvania, suffered dreadfully from the cold. Yet, stupefied by our loss, we consigned her in death to the one condition that pained her in life. There seemed to be no other choice.

The next morning, we drove to the funeral home. We were ushered into a room equipped with comfortable chairs and a conference table. Magazines featuring glossy photographs of burial urns and coffins were stacked at the center alongside a box of tissues. We learned that our mom had been transported to the county medical examiner's office to await an autopsy. Because she had died as a result of a fall—the one that came after that fatal step across my sister's kitchen in December— her death was deemed "accidental" and therefore warranted the invasive, humiliating procedure that is an autopsy.

"I'm afraid it's the law," replied the mortician's apprentice when we asked why. She was a pleasant young woman whose cheerfulness, I imagined, was the consequence of plying her trade in a subtropical land of blue skies and blooming hibiscus. Then she explained the cremation procedure: how the body would be covered by a cardboard canopy, placed on a conveyor belt, and then moved along into the fire. Once the body was in the furnace, the process would take three hours.

Our mother had wanted it this way, I kept reminding myself, even as the young woman was talking. Always beautiful and always vain, Mom had emphatically made it known that she did not want a wake, did not want people lining up to see her lying dead in a casket, and did not want her family and friends remarking on how "natural" and "lifelike" she seemed. (She knew she would be neither.) A wake was a humiliation, anathema to beauty, and she was having no part of it. Nor did she want her body buried beneath the ground. Next to cold, my mother had dreaded dark, enclosed places most. She would panic in elevators and highway tunnels. "It feels like the walls are closing in," she'd complain. "I can't breathe."

And yet *I* didn't want it this way. As events unfolded, Mom would wait two days for the medical examiner, who was "backed up" with a seeming excess of supposedly suspicious deaths. During those days, she languished in a body bag in a cooler—not only cold, but naked as well, since her hospital gown had been removed and no one had asked us to provide clothes. I didn't want her hidden, naked, and alone in cold, dark places. I didn't want her to be sliced by a circular saw and splayed on a table, her organs hefted and measured by some white-coated county coroner. And I didn't want her closed up quickly, zipped back into the body bag, and hauled off to another cooler where she'd wait to be dispatched to the crematorium. (The very use of the term "crematorium" in the same sentence with the word "mother" I still find disturbing. What words are further apart, both in meaning and in feeling?)

Instead, I wanted a mortician who loved his craft to work magic with my mother—to embalm her body, carefully and gently; to apply makeup and nail polish; to arrange her hair and dress her in her favorite suit. I wanted her placed in a mahogany coffin lined with silk the color of lilac. I wanted him, too, to practice the Sacrament of Beauty.

Most of all, I wanted a wake, a chance for her children and grandchildren to bear witness to the reality of her passing and to say our last farewells. Our brothers had not been present when our mother passed away; the wake would be their chance to pay their final respects. Also, my children had not visited my mother for several years, and much of the reason they were traveling long distances to Florida (from Minnesota, New York, and Belgium) was to see her, touch her, and be in her presence one last time.

Afterward, I wanted us all to accompany her blessed body—the one that carried her five children—to the church for Mass and, finally, to her resting place beside my father in St. Mary's Cemetery in Wilkes-Barre, Pennsylvania, where the two of them would await the Resurrection together. This is how Catholics wake and bury our loved ones. We have observed these rituals for centuries, and though they may fill us with desolation, they also grant us the consolation of having fulfilled our obligation to honor the body—accompanying our dead on their earthly pilgrimage as far as we possibly can and then placing them in holy ground, consecrated by the saints around them, for safekeeping.

But this is not what happened. Before we left the funeral home, the pleasant young woman invited us and any members of our family to return and see our mother one last time before the cremation, scheduled for Thursday. And yet, on Wednesday when we called to arrange this final visit, we were told that she had already been cremated. It seems they were less busy than they had anticipated, and so our mother's body had been dispatched and processed.

She was gone.

We children had a mixed reaction. One of my sisters was relieved that the burning, which we all dreaded, was over. We had, in fact, been invited to be present when her body passed through the fire, but we instinctively recoiled at this possibility. We were relieved that such a distasteful business was going to be handled by professionals. My other sister was disappointed—an agreement had been breached, and they did not grant us even the courtesy of a phone call to let us know this irrevocable process was about to begin.

But I was angry: angry to imagine my mother just waiting there, alone, like a piece of unclaimed baggage, and angry at my own lack of mindfulness, my failure to insist that her body be treated with dignity, regardless of her misguided wishes.

Yes, they were misguided—for I was convinced that when our mother envisioned the cremation process (if she envisioned it at all), she did not imagine a scenario that would leave us all feeling so empty and forlorn.

Yet even if she had—and even if she still would have chosen this route—I'm not at all sure I believe the wishes of the dead should take precedence over the wishes of those left behind. The rites we perform in the presence of the beloved's body are our gifts to the dead and to one another. They are the only means available to us to make the absurd, appalling, and enraging fact of death meaningful—the only means we have of asserting that life *matters*, the body *matters*, and our lived history together *matters*, both now and in the context of eternity.

In their marvelous book *The Good Funeral*, Thomas Long and Thomas Lynch delineate clearly the benefits accrued to the living by the traditional burial practices Christians have observed for centuries, as well as the reasons that modern methods of cremation are so problematic:

> "It is by bearing our dead from one station to the other—deathbed to parlor, parlor to altar, altar to the edge of eternal life—that we learn to bear death itself. By going the distance with them we learn to walk upright in the faith that God will take care of God's own, living and dead. . . . To the extent that cremation has become an accomplice in the out-of-sight and out-of-mind nature of memorial services, it is at cross-purposes with the life of faith and the mission of the church. The problem is not that we cremate our dead, but how ritually denatured, spiritually vacant, religiously timid, and impoverished we have allowed the practice to become. It is not *that* we do it, but *how* we do it that must be reconsidered."[1]

Our experience with Mom's cremation attests to the lack of any ceremonial, ritual, or sacramental element in this method of carrying out one of life's most important procedures: the disposal of our mother's body. We had elected to skip the stately procession, to avoid bearing the body from station to station, and instead allowed strangers to dispose of her without any aid or accompaniment.

If I had been more deliberate, I might have done things differently. I might have found some way, perhaps, for us to be present, both physically and spiritually, to my mother during her last hours on earth and to ground the experience in some kind of meaningful practice. We might have read some words, recited some prayers, sung some hymns, or brought some meaningful artifacts to accompany her into the fire. Unfortunately, though, when the reality of these omissions struck home, it was too late.

Three days later, we held a funeral Mass for my mother. Prayers were said, scripture read, bread blessed, and eulogies spoken. But heartfelt and faithful as these offices were, it seemed strange to be performing them in the absence of her body. It was as if she was not there.

THE SACRAMENT OF RECONCILIATION

For months after my mother's death, I regretted the fact that I did not honor her body. I tried to atone for this sin of omission in various ways. First, I brought her ashes to New York with me to reside in my home until the spring, when we could inter her remains in the earth of northeastern Pennsylvania, where she was born. The decision to bury her ashes itself was a departure from the plan our mother had outlined, but I had learned from one mistake I had made and was doing all I could to prevent making another.

About a year before she died, Mom told my sisters she wished to have her ashes scattered in the Florida Everglades—a place she had visited with Gene, her longtime friend and companion, in earlier, happier years. When my sisters told me this, I confess I was surprised. My grandfather had purchased a burial plot for both my mother and father decades ago in St. Mary's Cemetery. Over the years, we had buried my father there, my mother's parents, and several uncles, including her brother Sam. The idea that my mother was choosing to have her remains scattered in a lonely swamp instead of being buried alongside her beloved family members in a place where her children and grandchildren could visit her struck me as shortsighted at best and selfish at worst. Our mother had never been a person of good judgment, so I suppose this particular lapse should not have surprised me. In addition, the fact that she arrived at this decision in the grip of her grief over the loss of Gene and during a period when she was drinking heavily also suggested that she was not thinking clearly when she made this request. For these reasons and more, both my heart and my mind told me that honoring my mother's misguided request was not consonant with honoring my mother. Happily, my sisters and my brothers agreed with me, and the decision was made that we would arrange for her burial.

In the interim, while waiting for the spring thaw, having my mother's ashes in my house made me strangely happy. I would greet her every morning when I came downstairs. Whereas I had felt her absence at the funeral Mass, I now felt that she was *with* me in some elemental, essential way, and I considered myself honored and lucky to be in possession of the relics of our familial saint. As the fourth of five children—an inauspicious position in the birth order if ever there was one—I felt my mother was finally mine in a way she had never been before. The presence of her ashes also enabled me to honor her through small sacramental practices.

When I arrived home, I searched the attic and was fortunate to find a silver box in which I placed the plain, wooden container that the crematorium had provided for us. Then I placed her on a table in our living room, ringed by photographs of her at various stages of her life and of our family members. I placed flowers there as well—a spray of lilacs, smelling of spring—and arranged the dozens of Mass cards sent by kind friends around her as they arrived. Her makeshift altar was flanked by two bodega-bought candles bearing the image of St. Anthony, our Mom's go-to saint. Two rosaries were draped over her box—the glass beads, blessed by the pope, that she had bought in Rome many years ago, and the set of travel beads that she held in her hand in the hospice room as she left this world and moved on to the next.

This intentionality and makeshift sacramental practice—the morning greeting, replacing the spent flowers with fresh ones, and rearranging the Mass cards—helped heal my sense of failure as a daughter. I realized, in fact, with more than a little pain, that I was more present to my mother in death than I had been in life. I also knew that this period of daily conversation would not last. In a few months' time, my siblings and I would bury her ashes in the grave where her body was supposed to go. A hole would be dug near the gravestone we had selected and engraved, and a priest would read the gospel and lead us in prayer. The box containing her remains would be lowered into the hole she so dreaded, and the hole would be filled. And there—as ash, instead of bone and perishable flesh—she would begin to await the Resurrection with my father. I would have to give her up at last.

THE SACRAMENT OF POETRY (REPRISE)

The final rite of atonement I adopted was the one that came most naturally to me as a writer and a poet. Returning to the practice I had undertaken when she was undergoing surgery—and, truly, a practice I had been engaging in for years before that, though with less intensity—I wrote about my mother, compulsively, obsessively, possessively. I wrote poems about moments of our lives that I thought were lost, but which then returned to me: of helping her make spaghetti sauce in the kitchen of my childhood and of her calling me home to supper from the back-porch door. I wrote poems about our recent days and hours together, hoping to freeze those fleeting moments, to make the memory of them substantial so that they would not be lost in the unstoppable stream of time. And I wrote poems about my evolving sense of who my mother was. Somehow I was able to see her better after she was dead than I ever could when she was alive. She would come to me at the oddest moments during the day, and often in my dreams, sometimes telling me things that I needed to hear from her, but mostly remaining silent so that I had to imagine what she might be trying to say. One of these poems speaks, particularly, to the communication I craved so much but could no longer have.

Poem on Waking

Today I woke to talk to my mother.
Her face appeared, clean as a dream,
erased of age and any trace of grief,
my mother as I wanted her to be.

She seemed to long to speak to me of love,
and I of mercies I had lately learned.
Her eyes smiled, although her mouth stayed closed,
as if what *need* be, *might* be said through those.

I searched my purse and found my cell phone,
touched the icon box marked with her name—
then saw the stranger living in her house
and knew that she was gone, yet again.

The voice I'm waiting for, still unheard.
For all my life, not one more word.[2]

Poetry enabled me to comprehend, at least partially, the incomprehensible. It helped me to break the silence and to wrap my arms around this sudden absence at the center of my being. With rhythm and with rhyme I was able to exert some measure of control over the chaos of death. I would not be defeated by it, nor would my mother. Poetry gave me the wherewithal to tame the beast, lock it in a cage of language, and throw away the key.

THE SACRAMENT OF BURIAL

On May 24, 2010, my brothers and sisters flew to New York and came to my house, and we set out on the journey together by car to northeastern Pennsylvania. It took us several hours to drive the hundred-mile distance, and my sisters and I remarked on how beautiful and green the mountains in that part of the world are. (Though we had grown up there, we had forgotten.) We were also late for the ceremony. We had set out as a caravan, but my sisters and I followed a different set of directions to our destination. This resulted in our being delayed on the interstate on account of an accident. Our other family members called us repeatedly, urging us to hurry since the priest was waiting, but we knew the interment could not begin without us, for Mom's ashes were traveling with us in the back of my car. (We thought of her signature expression when we realized this: "I'm the important person here!"—the Sacrament of Humor asserting itself, yet again, even in such solemn circumstances.)

When we did at last arrive, all proceeded beautifully. The small crowd assembled around the grave, and the ceremony was brief and elegant. Most of our grief had been spent during the last few months. This felt like an occasion we had been looking forward to rather than one we dreaded. The gravesite was flanked by my mother's favorite floral arrangement, a bleeding heart, and baskets of flowers from friends and relatives. Mom's stone was in place, one we had chosen to match our father's; though, because his was so weathered after all his years of waiting, the two looked nothing alike. (This struck me as a poignant metaphor for the estrangement between my parents, who had not seen one another for almost half a century.) The gravediggers who cut the small hole in the ground stood aside, shovels in hand, shifting from foot to foot, as we prayed. When we finished, they gently and ceremoniously covered Mom's box with dirt. (We tipped them handsomely—twice—as our generous mother would have done. We wanted them to remember her.) And having accompanied her, at last, as far as we could, we left her in the care of the earth and the God who made it.

CODA

The daily wake I held for my mother, from the time I brought her to my home to the day of her interment, lasted 105 days, far beyond two or three nights, as is the custom. I talked to my mother on each one of those days, and I often asked her as she waited patiently on her altar, "Mom, though I failed in the duties of love at first, have I succeeded now? Have I not honored you, after all, in my fashion?"

Of course, I received no answer. Instead, she would smile at me from the photograph beside her silver box, a picture taken of her in her white Woolworth's uniform at age seventeen. In the portrait, a tiny, silver cross rests against her slender neck, and the words "Love, Marion" are signed across the bottom of the photo in her broad, familiar hand—two words that were written long before my birth, and yet, I believed then, and still do now, that somehow they were meant for me.

Epilogue

THE SACRAMENT OF MEMORY

Remember me when I am gone away.
Gone far away into the silent land.
—Christina Rossetti

In his essay "Sacraments," quoted in the Introduction, Andre Dubus claims that the sacraments are not seven in number but "seven times seventy." In choosing this number, Dubus wisely echoes Christ's words to Peter when the disciple asks him how many times he ought to forgive his brother who sins against him. Though they have each named the same finite number, Jesus does not suggest that we need to forgive our offenders only 490 times, nor does Dubus suggest that there are only 490 sacraments. To make this abundantly clear, Dubus adds to Christ's formula, "seven times seventy, *to infinity.*" The sacraments, then, like our capacity for forgiveness, cannot be counted, weighed, and hefted—both are numberless and immeasurable.

The infinite nature of sacrament is temporal as well. The sacraments we make in taking care of those we love do not stop when they die. We continue to care for the beloved in a way that is certainly different from ministering to bodily needs yet still fulfills the conditions of sacrament. In chapter 1, the meditation on the Sacrament of Speech concludes with a definition and an observation.

Sacrament is enacted ritual wherein the unseen is made visible, the unsayable is spoken, and the eternal is made manifest in the transitory world. All three of these conditions would be fulfilled, at various times, during Mom's forty-eight days in the ICU, nursing home, and hospice care. This sacramental practice, the attempt to heal disaster through redemptive acts of love, was set in motion by the split-second event of my mother's fall on December 16 at 5:00 p.m. in my sister's kitchen. It has yet to stop.

One of the surprises of the journey we have made in the years since my mother's illness and passing is that we do not have to stop caring for her, even though she is no longer with us. In fact, we find this impossible. The sacramental practice we perform in her absence most often is that of remembrance—holding her in our hearts and minds and making her present to ourselves and to others. We do this in any number of ways.

The Sacrament of Memory often takes the form of conscious actions, such as telling stories about Mom at family gatherings, quoting some of her memorable expressions, attending Mass on the anniversaries of her birth and death, visiting her grave, and writing about her. (Yes, even this book is a sacramental practice.) My sisters and I have also enjoyed a recently evolved sacramental practice—remembering my mother on Facebook on Mother's Day and other significant occasions by posting pictures of her, sharing a story or two, and publicly expressing our love for her and our grief at her loss. This latter form of the sacrament, made possible by the miracles of technology and social networking, is a particularly welcome gift, since it heals the geographical distance that separates us from one another and also allows us to invite other friends and family members to engage in the Sacrament of Memory with us. It is astonishing and gratifying to join with friends from places as far-flung as California, Florida, Minnesota, New York, Paris, and London in remembering Mom, celebrating her life, and collectively missing her.

The Sacrament of Memory, like many of the makeshift rituals explored in earlier chapters, may also take the form of unconscious, involuntary actions. For example, I dream about my mother on a regular basis, more than I ever did when she was alive. Although she is no longer here to guide me (and, truth be told, to chide me), it seems as if she has taken up residence in my consciousness and speaks to me from there. It is interesting that these are nearly always happy dreams. My mother appears as an altered version of herself, one that is more wise, more serene, more at peace with herself and those around her. We are at ease with one another in a way that we never were in life—a circumstance that fills me with hope and consolation.

Another involuntary sacramental ritual that unfolds on a regular basis occurs when I cook, especially when I prepare the dishes my mother taught me to make. Whenever I chop garlic and drop it into a skillet of sizzling olive oil, whenever I open a large can of plum tomatoes with my old-fashioned manual can opener, and whenever I shape meatballs and brown them in the pan, turning each carefully so it gets evenly cooked on each side, my mother is there with me. I feel her presence, her easy grace in the kitchen. She was not a precise, fussy cook but a brisk, competent one—able to field a phone call, keep an eye on a roaming toddler, and sing along with the Connie Francis song playing on the stereo, all while she made a fabulous meal. I have learned this from her, and when I cook, I reenact these rituals.

"These are just a few of many possible instances I might cite, and I'm sure my sisters could name others. The Sacrament of Memory takes many forms—"seven times seventy," one might say—and it serves as one of the most potent sources of consolation that we experience after losing those we love. Through these brief, fleeting moments, we come as close as we can to having our beloveds with us again. For this reason, though it is a sacrament we practice with sadness at times, we mostly practice it with pleasure.

It seems to me that the clearest analogy to this makeshift sacrament is the actual sacrament of Eucharist. When Christ breaks bread and offers wine to his disciples at the Last Supper, he issues a clear directive: "Do this in memory of me." Since that original event two centuries ago, the sacrament of Eucharist continues to invite and enable Jesus' followers to reenact the very same meal—to take bread in our hands, to taste wine on our tongues, and to take into ourselves (somehow) the body and blood of the Beloved. And we do all of this in the service of memory. Although the events that are memorialized in this familiar ritual entail sorrow—this is, in fact, the night before Christ's death—it is noteworthy that, in the language of the Mass, the Eucharist is described as a "celebration." And why wouldn't it be? The Eucharist reminds us of the events by which death is undone, by which mortal human beings are given the gift of immortality.

The Sacrament of Memory, like the sacrament of Eucharist—and like all of the sacraments we make in caring for those we love—is one more way of affirming life in the face of apparent death, of gaining glimpses of the eternal in the transitory world, and of practicing resurrection. Embracing our past and anticipating our future, memory is hopeful, limitless, and ongoing. It's no wonder it leads us to joy.

ACKNOWLEDGMENTS

I am very grateful to friends and colleagues who have assisted me in completing this book. First, my thanks must go to my editor, Lil Copan, who first invited me to take on the project of writing a prose meditation on the sacramental practice of accompanying my mother in her final illness. This book would not exist were it not for her creative energy and encouragement.

In addition, I am grateful to my colleagues at Fordham University's Curran Center for American Catholic Studies. To Christine Firer Hinze and Maria Terzulli, I am grateful for their enthusiasm about this project and for their patience and support during the process of preparing this manuscript.

I want to extend heartfelt thanks to those who offered invaluable encouragement at various stages of this project over the last few years, especially Alan Berecka, Pierce Butler, Maryanne Hannan, Peter Quinn, Peggy Steinfels, and Peter Steinfels.

I am grateful for the support I received from the Collegeville Ecumenical Institute's Ecclesial Writing Project in the form of a week's writing residency in the "Apart yet A Part" program. Inspired by my colleagues in the program and by our writing coach, Michael McGregor, I wrote the key chapter of the manuscript during my week there, and it changed the course of the book.

I'd like to express my deepest gratitude to my family, in particular to my husband, Brennan, for his love and long friendship and for his unfailing support and encouragement of my work. As ever, his fine ear and unerring eye have made this a better book. I am also fortunate in my sons, Charles, Patrick, and Will—discriminating readers who, happily, always manage to find something of value in their mother's writing.

Finally, I am grateful to my sisters, Charlene and Rose Ann, for their generous permission to share our story and for their kind attention and care in reading and commenting on the manuscript. In addition, I am grateful to my brothers, Gregory and Lou, for their steady presence and their unfailing love and support. I have been blessed to share the whole of my life with my brothers and sisters, and it is a pleasure and a privilege to acknowledge the debt of gratitude I owe them. This book is dedicated to them.

NOTES

INTRODUCTION

1. Andre Dubus, "Sacraments," in *Meditations from a Moveable Chair* (New York: Random House, 1998), 85.

2. Andrew Greeley, *The Catholic Imagination* (Berkeley: University of California Press, 1988), 1.

3. Andre Dubus, "On Charon's Wharf," in *Broken Vessels* (New York: Godine Publishers, 1991), 77.

1. THE SACRAMENT OF SPEECH

1. John Milton, *Paradise Lost*, in *Complete Poems and Major Prose by John Milton*, ed. Merritt Y. Hughes (New York: Hackett, 2003), 459.

2. Frank Kermode, *The Sense of an Ending* (London: Oxford University Press, 2000), 46.

2. THE SACRAMENT OF DISTANCE

1. Robert Frost, "Stopping by Woods on a Snowy Evening," in *The Collected Poems Complete and Unabridged: The Poetry of Robert Frost* (New York: Holt, Rinehart, and Winston, 1969), 224.

2. Emily Dickinson, *The Complete Poems of Emily Dickinson*, ed. Thomas H. Johnson (New York: Little, Brown, 1960), 35.

3. Dickinson, *The Complete Poems*, 63.

4. Denise Levertov, "A Poet's View," in *New and Selected Essays* (New York: New Directions, 1992), 243.

5. David Jones, "Art and Sacrament," in *Epoch and Artist*, ed. Harman Grisewood (London: Faber and Faber, 1952), 145–78.

6. Marilynne Robinson, *Gilead*, (New York: Picador, 2006), 19.

7. Robert Frost, "Letter to an Amherst Student," in *The Collected Prose of Robert Frost*, ed. Mark Richardson (Cambridge, MA: Belknap Press, 2010), 115.

8. William Blake, "The Marriage of Heaven and Hell," in *The Complete Poems* (New York: Penguin, 1988), 191.

9. Angela Alaimo O'Donnell, "A Blessing for My Mother," in *Waking My Mother* (Cincinnati: WordTech Press, 2013), 17.

3. THE SACRAMENT OF BEAUTY

1. John O'Donohue, *Beauty: The Invisible Embrace* (New York: HarperCollins, 2004), 13.

2. Dubus, "On Charon's Wharf," in *Broken Vessels*, 79.

3. O'Donnell, "Watching *Dirty Dancing* with My Mother," in *Waking My Mother*, 34.

4. THE SACRAMENT OF HUMOR

1. Ernest Kurtz, *The Spirituality of Imperfection* (Collegeville, MN: Liturgical Press, 1999), 190.

2. Peter Berger, *Redeeming Laughter: The Comic Dimension of Human Experience* (Berlin: De Gruyter Press, 1997), 205.

3. Erasmus, *In Praise of Folly*, quoted in Berger, *Redeeming Laughter*, 20.

4. Jürgen Moltmann, *The Coming of God* (Minneapolis: Fortress Press, 2004), 339.

5. THE SACRAMENTS OF THE CELL PHONE AND THE WHEELCHAIR

1. Dubus, "Sacraments," in *Meditations*, 98–99.
2. Dubus, "Bodily Mysteries," in *Meditations*, 101.

6. THE SACRAMENT OF WITNESS

1. O'Donnell, "Real Presence," in *Waking My Mother*, 38.

7. THE SACRAMENT OF HONOR

1. Thomas Long and Thomas Lynch, *The Good Funeral* (Louisville, KY: Westminster John Knox Press, 2013), 186–87.

2. O'Donnell, "Poem on Waking," in *Waking My Mother*, 70.

Founded in 1865, Ave Maria Press,
a ministry of the Congregation of
Holy Cross, is a Catholic publishing
company that serves the spiritual and
formative needs of the Church and its
schools, institutions, and ministers;
Christian individuals and families; and
others seeking spiritual nourishment.

For a complete listing of titles from

Ave Maria Press

Sorin Books

Forest of Peace

Christian Classics

visit www.avemariapress.com

ave maria press® / Notre Dame, IN 46556
A Ministry of the United States Province of Holy Cross